Peace
After Your
Broken
Relationship

By: Evangelist Bill Carter
Copyright 2009

This book is about some of the things
that keep us from having peace
when we have or had a broken relationship.
These writings will help you,
enter into another relationship.
And give yourself a real chance to change
and have a greater life.
We as single adults should have knowledge
and understanding of the hurt and pain
that comes after a relationship falls apart.
And to have the courage to get back into another
relationship!
I have placed key Bible verses (KJV) with subject of interest
for you to stand on, as you recover.
As you recover, find a new relationship.

Printed in Victoria, BC, Canada.

ISBN: 978-1-4269-2521-4

Library of Congress Control Number: 2009914224

*Our mission is to efficiently provide the world's finest, most comprehensive book publishing
service, enabling every author to experience success. To find out how to publish your book, your
way, and have it available worldwide, visit us online at www.trafford.com*

Trafford rev. 3/18/2010

 www.trafford.com

North America & international
toll-free: 1 888 232 4444 (USA & Canada)
phone: 250 383 6864 ♦ fax: 812 355 4082

FORWARD

Many books have been written on the message of the Bible, but this one is in many ways unique. For those who truly love the word of God. You will find these chapters both a challenge and inspiration.

The author is a dedicated layperson, who for years has had a prayerful urge to dig deeper into the writings for this book. This book is written for all single adults / youth and will give knowledge to those who are seeking peace from their broken relationship.

Not only for single adults and the youth, but those with more experience, such as group leaders, ministers, ministry, church, Bible teacher and layperson; will appreciate the way these chapters link up with strong scripture passages. Which are illuminating statements from the inspired writing of the Bible! While his thoughts are deep, he presents them in a lucid winning way.

As this book now leaves for the publishers, we believe the fulfillment of God's promise will be apparent to all that seek him; in love of the truth as it is in Christ Jesus! May the Holy Spirit move each reader to dig deeper into the material of this book of truth; in scripture which is indeed the love of Jesus Christ. To his people, may it bring you a breath of fresh air from heaven! May heavenly sunshine flood the chambers of your mind and above all may Jesus Christ become a vital part of your inmost being.

Dr. Ed Davis N.D.
Medical Missionary Ministries
Breaman, KY

There is someone out there looking for someone like you.

About the author: Evangelist Bill Carter

I have studied single adult ministries teachings for a few years. I have spent a lot of time listening to people talk about their relationships and helped a lot of people get over the hurt of a broken relationship. I have always point them toward Jesus and the Church. This book has some writings about my mistakes and my past relationships I was in.

I wrote the 1st part of this book from how I felt over a few broken relationships.
And how other people felt as well.
The 2nd part of this book I wrote when I was in Iraq working with our great military.
These writings are to help people change,
to better one's self, in love, relationships and companionships.
The 3rd part of this book are teachings I done on different subjects,
and some writings from when I was in Iraq.

I took the time to place key Bible verse to help you find the truth. Life is a long walk. If people, would walk with the word of God in their hearts, life would be so much easier.

If you have a friend that you can't help!
This book may help them find a path to a new beginning.

Some of this book was written while on base
At:
COB Speicher / Tikrit, Iraq
12/23/06 to 6/5/07

This book was written to make you think about
Relationships, past, present and future!

May this book bless you and all who read these pages!
I'm asking that the churches open their doors to single adult ministry
And use this book as a teaching!

Special thanks to: Pastor Dr. Ed Davis & Pastor David Atherton
In all they have done to support me for all these years.
Edited and proof read by:
Pastor Dr. Ed Davis, Pastor David Atherton and Evangelist Bill Carter all from Kentucky

Index

PART THREE

Part Four

First part of the break up is a time of prayer

You are hurt and full of anxiety. *Hurt is a small word compared to how we can really feel.* Your hurt may include: *anger, loss, loneliness, rejection, guilt, revenge, shame, depression, fear, bitterness and so on.* But what about when we are not trusting God our Father, not going to Church, loss of faith, not reading our Bible and not praying. **Can this happen to a real Christian? Yes, it can, and has.** What should a Christian do if this starts? The first step is to pray, if you don't you may fall into more doubt. That's the last thing you need when you are already hurting from a broken relationship. ***Living in doubt is like living upside down.***

Psalm 34:15-18 The *eyes of the Lord are upon the righteous, and his ears are open unto their cry. Vs. 16: The face of the Lord is against them that do evil, to cut off the remembrance of them from the earth.* ***Vs. 17: The righteous cry, and the Lord heareth, and delivereth them out of all their troubles. Vs. 18: The Lord is nigh unto them that are of a broken heart; and saveth such as be of a contrite spirit.***

1Thessalonians 5:17 *Pray without ceasing.*

Ephesians 6:18 ***Praying always with all prayer and supplication in the spirit, and watching thereunto with all perseverance and supplication for all saints;***

When you are hurting from a broken relationship, you should always start praying. Why, to keep yourself from getting into the flesh and to fight the attacks of Satan. When we are hurting we will fight with the flesh and all the attacks of Satan. Therefore if we pray as we hurt, we have a God given chance to recover in the spirit of the Lord. I have prayed hours on end, days and for months. *In most books that I read and study about broken relationship and single adult ministry, most of the writers stated that it might take up to six months or years to overcome a broken heart.* That is why we must pray and seek peace from our Father God. If you don't, you may lose your faith, walk, and trust in our Lord Jesus Christ. All of this can happen from a broken heart. The Bible teaches us to pray for healing. This may be the only way to get over the hurt and anxiety. You will remain in that stage of hurting until you give all the hurt to Jesus Christ. One may ask, how hard is that; *hard as we make it!* ***That's why it's between you and your prayer life. We must lay our hurt down at the feet of Jesus!*** This faith will give you a chance to have your life renewed by Jesus. That is the only true way to overcome hurt and anxiety. Yes, this may still take awhile. Yes, there will be small steps in your recovery. Yes, from time to time you may fall back. But, it's up to you to get back up; no one can do this for you at all. **But note this: (We can't change the will of some one. Don't get into this kind of prayer. Yes, you can ask God to speak to them, but leave it at that.) God our Father has given everyone a free will. So don't try to pray into that area).** *It will only prolong your hurt if you try to change the will of someone.* One other way to get over the hurt is to pray for that person who has left you. Why not! This will

make you feel a little better as well! Pray that God will forgive them and bless them. Remember when you pray a blessing over someone's life God will see your love and God will bless you. ***Remember not all relationships, will end up in friendship, but you must be a Christian and forgive them. That's what Jesus would do!***
You must be able to give to receive. So give a prayer of blessing to them that hurt you! For the Lord hears our prayers. **That's why we must pray and pray we must!** Prayer can do a lot. It heals and blesses. These are just two things prayer can do for you, so use prayer time for this reason. ***The storm you're going through is what God will use to save you and bless you!***

Psalm 116:17 *I will offer to thee the sacrifice of thanksgiving, and will call upon the name of the Lord.*

I'm still in love with the other person

This is one of the hardest parts to get over. We try to hang on to a relationship with the love we have for the other person. It has been said, "if you really love someone you will always have love for them". ***You must learn to change and control your love for them.*** That alone will take time. We as Christians should never hate anyone at all. If we hate we have judged that person. That is not Christ like at all! We must forgive, in order to have peace with God our Father!

Matthew 5:7 *Blessed are the merciful: for they shall obtain mercy.*

If you start feeling that you have hate growing in you; you must repent and be merciful In doing this you will have a greater chance for recovery in this broken relationship! I need to say this one more time. ***We will have to learn to change our love for that person and to control that feeling in order to be healed!*** **Change your love to compassion!**

The Christian Virtues
Colossians 3:12-14 *Put on therefore, as the elect of God, holy and beloved, bowels of mercies, kindness, humbleness of mind, meekness, long-suffering; Vs. 13: Forbearing one another, and forgive one another, if any man have a quarrel against any: even as Christ forgave you, so also do ye. Vs.14: And above all these things put on charity, which is the bond of perfectness.*

We as Christians would gain so much if we would live by these few verses. This is how we can overcome the love we have in a broken relationship. Go back and read these few verses again to place them into your heart.

Dealing with rejection

This is one more area you will have to deal with. This will be just as hard as any other area that you will face in a broken relationship. You must keep your confidence about yourself and let God be God. This will be hard to do, that's why we must pray to rebuild our life. If you lose your confidence you will lose your peace and joy.

Hebrew 10:35 *Cast not away therefore your confidence, which hath great recompense of reward.*

Hebrew 3:14 *For we are made partakers of Christ, if we hold the beginning of our confidence steadfast unto the end;*

Christians without confidence may enter into a backsliding state of living. That is why we must study the Bible to keep our confidence in our Lord Jesus Christ. If you know the word of God you can pray from the word of God. I've been in broken relationships that have hurt me. Praying always helps.

Losing confidence will affect you as a Christian. That's why we must know the word of God and pray every time we start to hurt or lose our confidence. ***Remember the truth will set you free. Those who are free in Christ are free indeed! Amen!***

Dealing with your anger

You will have to deal with your anger. Don't let this grow at all in you! *Let me ask you this, who is to blame in a past relationship? No one! This may be hard for you to accept, but it's true.* Marriage may be a little different but still stay away from anger. Anger can kill you and your health. Anger will cause you to sin and cause you great pain. Anger only hurts! Just forgive and rebuild your life. Anger will only bring you to a lower level of life. Anger will keep you hurting longer then you need to. **Anger needs to be kept under control!**

Psalm 37:8 Cease *from anger, and forsake wrath: fret not thyself in any wise to do evil.*

Proverbs 14:17 *He that is soon angry dealeth foolishly: and a man (or woman) of wicked devices is hated.*

These two verses tell us, to cease from anger and that anger is foolish. I know this area of a broken relationship is tough and hard to overcome. But be Christ like. When you feel anger in your heart, you need to start to pray. Don't let Satan play with your mind or your life.

Attitude

I do believe you will have to get past hurt, rejection, and anger to get your Christian attitude back. This is a part of your confidence as well. Day by day you will grow stronger, that is one more reason to overcome anger as well. We will always have to grow, change, and adjust our attitude. Day by day and year by year we will have to do this.

Acts 24:16 *And herein do I exercise myself, to have always a conscience void of offense toward God, and toward man.*

Colossians 3:15 *And let the peace of God rule in your hearts, to thee which also ye are called in one body; and be ye thankful.*

You know if your attitude has changed. I know it will take time to adjust and over come. That is why we must pray for peace. ***As long as you are angry, your attitude will not change.*** We must keep these verses in our heart and mind. Stop here and pray that Jesus will give you a great attitude!

Anxiety

I can't write enough about this, though I will keep it short. We can carry anxiety around for a long time. If you were in love, there will be anxiety in your life after a break up. How can you overcome anxiety? A lot of work will have to be applied here. Work out, eating right, resting, forgiving, praying, studying your Bible, or just take up a new hobby. But this will be left up to you. But stay off the alcohol, street drugs, drug abuse and self pity. Set small goals, don't go and make big decisions. Do things for yourself that make you feel good and remember to take your time in rebuilding your life. Start small as you put your life back together. Tell your family, loved ones and friends that you can only deal with this one day at a time, until you are healed.

Crying is good, but you may need to control this at times. The more you control your feelings the faster you can overcome some if not all of this anxiety. You must keep praying and keep your faith in God. If you don't have faith in God what is your faith? Anxiety will cause you to have an unsound mind.

1 Peter 5:6-7 *Humble yourselves therefore under the mighty hand of God, that he may exalt you in due time: Vs. 7 Casting all your care upon him; for he careth for you.*

Proverbs 3:5-6 *Trust in the Lord with all thine heart; and lean not unto thine own understanding. Vs. 6 In all thy ways acknowledge him, and he shall direct thy paths.*

Romans 8:28 *And **we know that all things work together for good to them that love God**, to them who are the called according to his purpose.*

Philippians 4:19 *But my God shall supply all your need according to his riches in glory by Christ Jesus.*

Fear

This can destroy the greatest of men and women. Our fear should be in the Lord Jesus Christ and God our Father only. My two greatest fears are being alone and growing old by my self, but I still have God and my prayer life. Fear not for God our Father is always with us as a Christian. ***We need to learn how to change fear to trusting in the Lord Jesus Christ.*** If we would only do this we would become stronger for the glory of God. But how do we overcome this fear factor? By facing the truth, the truth will set us free in due time! The real question is can you be free in Christ? *We need to check where our faith is, it should be in Christ Jesus and him alone!*

Psalm 27:1   *The Lord is my light and my salvation: whom shall I fear? The Lord is the strength of my life; of whom shall I be afraid?*

Psalm 34:4 *I sought the Lord, and he heard me, and delivered me from all my fears.*

Isaiah 41: 10 *Fear thou not; for I am with thee: be not dismayed; for I am thy God: I will strengthen thee; yea, I will help thee; yea, I will uphold thee with the right hand of my righteousness.*

2Timothy 1:7 *For God hath not given us the spirit of fear; but of power, and of love, and of a sound mind.*

Hebrews 13:6 *So that we may boldly say, The Lord is My Helper, And I Will Not Fear What Man Shall Do Unto me.*

Bitterness

This will cause you to build unwanted walls. ***These walls you build will be the same walls you will have to tear down and take to the dump.*** *That's a lot of labor; you may have to go to the dump a few times in order to get rid of this trash!* Walls of bitterness are of judgment; this will cause you to fail at a God given relationship. ***(People will make mistakes; we are not perfect). If you have someone who is making mistakes in a relationship, they may be trying to learn how to have a relationship with you.***

Bitterness will become a stronghold in your life,
if you choose to keep bitterness in your heart.

Remember bitterness is not peace or joy. More so it's not the will of God our father. Bitterness will kill your life and all your happiness. That is a real fact of life.

Ephesians 4:31-32 *Let all bitterness, and wrath, and anger, and clamor, and evil speaking, be put away from you, with all malice: Vs. 32 be ye kind one to another, tenderhearted, forgiving one another, even as God for Christ's sake hath forgiven you.*

Hebrews 12:14-15 *Follow peace with all men, and holiness, without which no man shall see the Lord: Vs.15: Looking diligently lest any man fail of the grace of God; lest any root of bitterness springing up trouble you, and thereby many be defiled;*

Romans 12:21 *Be not overcome of evil, but overcome evil with good.*

Guilt

This is an area where we all can fall into without good reason. We will blame ourselves when we have no reason to blame ourselves. What if it just didn't work out, or the truth just came out. We only date to see if it can turn into something more than dating. **(*I need to point this out, don't ever mislead someone!*)**

This is hard to understand at times. *If it doesn't work out it's really no one's fault.* We should realize and understand if it doesn't work out, it's for the best. I've allowed myself to be hurt after a relationship. Yes, I even blamed myself, but what for? I tried and gave my best. If we are trying to do the right things and it doesn't work out remember you gave it your best shot. *I believe when you have love in your heart, it's a natural emotion to carry the blame and guilt.* Is there any good in this? Maybe to grow and to become a better person! **This does teach one thing; don't mislead anyone at all, including yourself**. I can only speak to you about this and it's up to you to understand, don't blame yourself in a broken relationship. We must remember to forgive as well. *Grow from this and seek another relationship if you want to be married!* Let's look at a few Bible verse.

John 14:26-27 *But the Comforter, which is the Holy Ghost, whom the Father will send in my name, he shall teach you all things, and bring all things to your remembrance, whatsoever I have said unto you. Vs. 27 Peace I leave with you, my peace I give unto you: not as the world giveth, give I unto you. Let not your heart be troubled, neither let it be afraid.*

Psalm 32:1 *Blessed is he (she) whose transgression is forgiven, whose sin is covered.*

Romans 8:1-2 *There is therefore now no condemnation to them which are in Christ Jesus, who walk not after the flesh, but after the Spirit. Vs. 2: For the law of the Spirit of life in Christ Jesus hath made me free from the law of sin and death.*

2 Chronicles 30:9 *For if ye turn again unto the LORD, your brethren and your children shall find compassion before them that lead them captive, so that they shall come again into this land: for the LORD your God is gracious and merciful, and will not turn away his face from you, if ye return unto him.*

Loneliness

This is where we can enter into a false relationship. I know I would like to have a long-term relationship that leads toward marriage. Therefore I do try to find a relationship on that basis! It's hard for me, or anyone to be alone. One cause of a "wrong relationship" is loneliness. Why? Our relationship has failed, and now we are alone. Loneliness may place you in a false relationship, do not allow yourself to enter into a false relationship. Few, if anyone really enjoys being alone. The fact is loneliness is hard for all of us.

Loneliness can lead to sin, and a cold heart! Being alone can hurt very deeply! This is where we need the church, fellowship and good friends! How do we overcome this loneliness? Try to find a Christian singles group is one way. Go to school, fix your home, work on your yard, but do something! Loneliness is real and you will have to find your own way out of this. As you rebuild your life, loneliness will leave. You must stay busy doing things for yourself and others.
In order to have something you must take action, set goals and have faith!

John 14:1 *If ye shall ask any thing in my name, I will do it.*

John 14:18 *I will not leave you comfortless: I will come to you*

Matthew 28:20 *Teaching them to observe all things whatsoever I have commanded you: and lo, I am with you always, even unto the end of the world. Amen.*

Genesis 28:15 *And, behold, I am with thee, and will keep thee in all places whither thou goest, and will bring thee again into this land; for I will not leave thee, until I have done that which I have spoken to thee of.*

I want to have a prayer for all those that are lonely: *Father God this hour, send someone into this person's life. It could be someone from the past or someone they haven't met just yet. Father, bless this person all the days of their life. Father, this person would be stronger if they had someone that you have sent. So send them O Lord, even this hour. We ask this in the name of Jesus Christ, Amen!*

Make a list of things you can do to keep you active.

Revenge

I'm going to keep this short, and allow you to search yourself. We as Christians should love everyone, everyday! **Revenge belongs to God only!** *Revenge is judgment, we shouldn't judge; that belongs to Jesus Christ and Him alone*! I only want to address this from Bible verses so you will have a greater understanding. **In doing this, I hope you will find peace in our Lord Jesus Christ forever more.**

Romans 12:19 *Dearly beloved, avenge not yourselves, but rather give place unto wrath: for it is written,* **VENGEANCE IS MINE; I WILL REPAY, saith the Lord.**

Hebrews 10:30-31 *For we know him that hath said,* **VENGEANCE BELONGETH UNTO ME, I WILL RECOMPENSE, saith the Lord. And again, THE LORD SHALL JUDGE HIS PEOPLE.** *Vs. 31: It is a fearful thing to fall into the hands of the living God.*

Matthew 6:14-15 For if ye forgive men (or women) their trespasses, your heavenly Father will also forgive your trespasses Vs.15: But if ye forgive not men (or women) their trespasses, neither will you Father forgive your trespasses.

Leviticus 19:18 Thou shalt not avenge, nor bear any grudge against the children of thy people, but thou shalt love thy neighbor as thyself: I am the LORD.

Deuteronomy 32:35 To me (the LORD) belongeth vengeance, and recompense; their foot shall slide in due time: for the day of their calamity is at hand, and the things that shall come upon them make haste.

1 Thessalonians 5:15 See that none render evil for evil unto any man; but ever follow that which is good, both among yourselves, and to all men.

Shame

Shame is much like the feeling of guilt. When you are going through shame, remember, you are still loved by God our Father. When a relationship is messed up; by being misunderstood or saying the wrong things, you may feel shame. If you are ashamed of your sins or past, you may never grow out of this area; until you repent. I don't know how many or just who might read this, but I want to share a prayer here. Shame can undercut even our best efforts to walk with God.

Heavenly Father, help us to get over this shame. For I know myself what this feels like, take this away with your great love and bring forth a blessing in our life. Fill us with a new life in Christ. Bring the happiness we need, to live a great life as a Christian. I ask this in

the name of Jesus Christ, Amen!
Go back to worshiping God Our Father. Increase your prayer life and be free of this shame.

Romans 10:11 *For with the heart man (woman) believeveth unto righteousness; and with the mouth confession is made unto salvation.*

Depression

There are a lot of good books written on this subject. No one really has the answer to this at all. Everyone experiences depression so differently, so this is what makes it hard to overcome. But I really believe loneliness plays a real big part here; as well as ending a relationship. The more depressed we become the more we seem to want to be alone. So I really think we need to take the battle to the area that may be causing us to be depressed. Here are five things you should work on if you are having a hard time overcoming this depression. *Keep busy, don't allow yourself to just sit around at all! Set small goals, you may not be in a position to set large goals, just take it easy! Eat right this is a must, don't eat junk foods at all; watch your sugar in take as well! Working out will help you fight back! One of the greatest things you can do is to do something for yourself, (anything). Treat yourself to something nice!*
If you are in the ministry and you are really getting depressed, take a break from your work until you have overcome this. Don't take on any more responsibility than you have to, slow down till you recover. We must, allow ourselves time! **If you really get depressed, seek help always! Remember this; you owe it to yourself to get help! Depression should be taken seriously, get help sooner rather than later.**

Isaiah 26: 3 *Thou wilt keep him in perfect peace, whose mind is stayed on thee: because he trusteth in thee.*

Isaiah 40:29 *He giveth power to the faint; and to them that have no might he increaseth strength.*

1 John 4:4 *Ye are of God, little children, and have overcome them: because greater is he that is in you, than he that is in the world*

Life at times is tough and the hurt is real. *But in order to find a real life, we must believe and walk in the will of God our Father every day. Yes, you may have to build up to this level in God, but in time you can do this if you press on. The more you know the word of God the greater chance you have in your recovery. This is a fact for all Christians! Studying the word of God will give you insight into what you need to pray for, every time you pray!* Don't forget to pray every time you feel depressed.

Thanksgiving

This may sound easy to do, but in a real fight for your life this will become tough to do. I want to tell you, this is a must for anyone who is in a spiritual battle! When we enter into thanksgiving, we are at the place where God wants us to be. As tough as this can be, remember this is the place God wants you to be! So do this for yourself and God. The blessing will come if you stay in a state of thanksgiving. I aways start noticing a change when I do this. You need to do this for three to four weeks in order to see a blessing come out of this type of prayer. *I aways have said why did I wait so long in doing this prayer of thanksgiving? Maybe we need to walk through the healing processes in order to pray like this. But thanksgiving is a part of healing, Amen! We should awaken everyday to give thanks to our Lord Jesus Christ!*

1 Thessalonians 5:18 *In every thing give thanks: for this is the will of God in Christ Jesus concerning you.*

Psalm 95:2 *Let us come before his presence with thanksgiving, and make a joyful noise unto him with psalm.*

Psalm 100: 4-5 *Enter into his gates with thanksgiving, and into his courts with praise: be thankful unto him, and bless his name.* **Vs. 5: For the Lord is good; his mercy is everlasting; and his truth endureth to all generations.**

Read: Psalm 136

Self control

Here is one area that can cause you a lot of problems, for the rest of your life. That is why we must be in control of our flesh everyday! We as Christians should never want to harm anyone. **Our father God is the avenger, don't forget this.** We as Christians, should never judge anyone, for it is written! *You don't need trouble on your hands.* We can have a bad behavior because of our imagination. *Your imagination will and can send you down the road of sin. If you are a Christian you will need to repent from issues.* Our imagination can happen faster than anyone can recover from! *In self-control we must control our IMAGINATION always. That is why we as Christians should never judge or take revenge. This belongs to God, not us! When we leave issue in the hands of God; God will take care of the issues. Believe me, I know. God doesn't allow someone to misuse his elect. People who do this will usually become sick or misplaced in life. I've seen this happen too often! So, just give it to God. God knows best!* It's a rewarding and a learning experience to learn how to stay in self-control, but this is a mark of a great Godly person. Most people don't believe that God is the one who gets revenge!

Psalm26:1-2 *Judge me, O lord; for I have walked in mine integrity: I have trusted also in the LORD; therefore I shall not slide. Vs. 2: Examine me, O LORD, and prove me, try my reins and my heart.*

Galatians 5:22-23 *But the fruit of the spirit is love, joy, peace, long-suffering, gentleness, goodness, faith, Vs.23: Meekness, temperance: against such there is no law.*

James 1:12 *Blessed is the man that endureth temptation: for when he is tried, he shall receive the crown of life, which the Lord hath promised to them that love him.*

Gossip

We shouldn't be doing this as Christians. Sometimes getting advice is like sitting a trap for yourself. Your friends can be the ones who cause a bad break up, not the person you are seeing. We shouldn't speak to friends as though they have all the answers. That belongs to God! *Here's how gossip happens: "Bill said this… what do you think about that…and what should I do." You may have just sat at the table of gossip and caused someone to have passed judgment on that person.* Now take a deeper look at this. What if the other person in your relationship was trying to communicate something that you misunderstood, and you destroyed what God was building because of your friends' ill advice! Put your cares on God, not on others! (Pray when you don't understand something the other person in your relationship was trying to communicate. That person may have been right or just said something that you misunderstood or did not know.) You will need to go back and correct this, for this is a type of judgment. If you don't, you and those involved may be judged by God himself. Don't allow yourself to destroy what God is doing in your life! *We need to be careful whom we share information with. They may give you their advice and be so completely wrong. That's a fact of life and this will destroy people's life.* LOOK AT THIS: *A lady that I was seeing asked me what I thought of so and so boyfriend for leaving her friend. She then went on to tell me what was going on. I told her that this was a one sided story, because I didn't know his side. It takes two, not just one side of the story to form a good opinion about a situation. After saying that I needed both sides of the story, I was judged by my friend for not taking sides.* **Who was right?** But yet we will believe someone's opinion and stay away from the truth. **God forbid!** These types of people often GOSSIP, and it is deeply embedded into their lives. THEY ARE SINNING, AND DON'T EVEN KNOW IT! THEY CAN DESTROY EVERYTHING IN THEIR PATH! Let me say this: **They may be living in hell, always having troubles, always trying to give advice or get advice, just so they can have attention or control!**

THEY DON'T CARE WHAT THEY SAY IN ORDER
TO DESTROY SOMETHING GOOD OR GOD SENT.

So be careful about getting advice from your friends; it may be a sin!
That is why we should pray, forgive and try to understand!
Gossiping and judgment go hand in hand!
Advice is something to use caution with while listening to.

15

If you seek advice to control someone's life, you are in the wrong.

Proverbs 20 :19 _He that goeth about as a talebearer revealeth secrets: therefore meddle not with him that flattereth with his (her) lips._

Proverbs 11:13 _A talebearer revealeth secrets: but he that is of a faithful spirit concealeth the matter._

Psalm 34:13 _Keep thy tongue from evil, and thy lips from speaking guile._

James 1:26 _If any man (women) among you seem to be religious, and bridleth not his tongue, but deceiveth his own heart, this man's religion is vain._

Assurance

I just want to speak from my point of view on this. When we are in love and the relationship comes apart, for whatever reason, we may or will blame God for this. I have done this as a Christian, but I was wrong! But what happens when we pull away from our Christian life and God? It becomes a hell on earth for us as Christians. Why? We have left God out of our life.

Therefore instead of blaming God we should rest in the Lord. Why do we forget to do this? **_Now where is our real assurance? It's in God our Father, Jesus, the Holy Spirit, the Bible, Church, and our Christian life. That is where our real assurance is, not blaming God!_** That's why we may need to take a rest in Christ. For over five months I didn't write anything. Why, because I blamed God over a broken relationship. Then the spirit of the Lord spoke to me about writing this book on broken relationships. I didn't write until the spirit of God moved me. Why? God knew I needed to move on. Writing this book helped me to understand my past.

So I said that to say this. **_If you or I stop being a Christian, what's left?_** We as Christians should keep our relationship alive in Christ Jesus! There is no other place to be in our assurance, than with our Lord Jesus Christ!

John 3:36 **_He that believe on the Son hath everlasting life:_** _and he that believe not the Son shall not see life; but the wrath of God abideth on him._

1 John 3:19 _And hereby we know that we are of the truth, and shall assure our hearts before him._

Hebrews 10:22 Let us draw near with a true heart in full assurance of faith, having our hearts sprinkled from an evil conscience, and our bodies washed with pure water.

Speaking openly

Now that I have written, on just a few subjects; I feel a need to speak and write openly to you, *about the pain, hurt and still being in love, after a broken relationship*. I deeply feel for you or anyone who has to walk through this part of recovery. There are no words to say to overcome this other than **time, forgiveness and understanding.** You may carry this type of pain for some time. I'm trying to minister to you as someone who has gone through this, and I have. I know about the pain, hurt and still being in love. It's real and deep; this is a part of your heart. At this point, only you can overcome this. You must realize it's going to take time and may be a lot of time. But note this, when we are hurting we can reach out in the wrong direction. This will only cause us to prolong the hurt. When you are dwelling on a past relationship; staying at home alone, drinking, using drugs, and feeling sorry for yourself. Not wanting to go places like church around your family, or just giving up on life. How can anyone get over this issue, living like this? You must make yourself get up and find your way in life. It takes a lot of work to be happy. Yes, it is up to you to take action!

It could take up to six months or years. *If you grow into love, you're going to have to grow out of love, and that takes time, forgiveness and understanding.* <u>You and these three things are the key to getting over a broken relation.</u> This is hard to do, but it's up to you to do this. <u>**One word of advice, get over a relationship before you get into another relationship.**</u> *Don't just jump back into another relationship. At least take three months or more before you start another relationship.* Allow adequate time for healing, before moving on to another relationship. Yes, go out as friends but don't become involved to a point where you become intimately involved.

<u>**Psalm 147:3**</u> *He healeth the broken in heart, and bindeth up their wounds.*

Sin Factor in Single Adults

I feel a real need to be open here, which may cause you and me to repent! *As I write I stand before God My Father and you as my Brother and Sister in Christ*. It is hard for single adults to have a long-term relationship without having sex. We, who have been married or exposed to sex, find this real hard to overcome. **Please understand this doesn't give us a license to sin at all.** We can read about this in the book of Romans and Paul's writings! I pray that God our Father will forgive each and every one of us that this has happened to. I pray that God will forgive you, them and me. *You may think the worst of me in this part of my writing, but we, as Christians need to be forgiven. Not only by Jesus, but also by the Christian Family!* **For we are sinners only saved by the grace of our Lord Jesus Christ!**

I do believe that sin does separate us from God, for it is written in the Bible! I'm not afraid to say that the sexual sin factor is at 80% or more, among the Christian single adults! You as adults should try six months, a year, or even four or five years without sex.

I know how tough this is, that's why we shouldn't judge one another. Leave this up to Jesus and him alone. For if you think you are better than this type of sinner. **I will ask you to talk about your sins for five minutes out loud to your Christian Family.** *Where would you stand if you did this? We only would ask to be forgiven! So, I'm asking you that have sexual sins, asks right now that Jesus would forgive all single adults.*
When we have sex outside of marriage this is where the peace of God will leave the relationship you're in. **We as adults will have sex mostly for two reasons, lust and loneliness. They both seem to condemn single adults.**

Hebrews 8:12 *For I will be merciful to their unrighteousness, and their sins and their iniquities will I remember no more.*

1 John 1:8-9 *If we say that we have no sin, we deceive ourselves, and the truth is not in us. Vs.9: If we confess our sins, he is faithful and just to forgive us our sins, and to cleanse us from all unrighteousness.*

A prayer for sexual sins

Father God, which is in heaven. Please forgive all single adults (and me) that have committed sexual sins and those who keep repeating this sin! We know that we don't have a license to sin. But I (we) failed in this area of the flesh; our flesh has became weak by lust and loneliness. This is where I (we) have really failed. Father I stand before you and my brothers and sisters confessing and asking for forgiveness; that you can only give. Father, send me my spouse and to all the single adults brothers send them their wives, and for all of the singles sisters send them their husband. Father I'm asking that you forgive my brothers and sisters. Teach us as a man to be spiritual leaders and the women to be a great wife. Father it's time to raise up the family God for all your glory! I'm asking that the Holy Spirit would go forth and protect and send their soul mates to each and everyone that hears or reads this prayer.
I ask this in the name of Jesus Christ our Lord!

Don't Judge Single Adults

It's with my heart that I ask you to keep reading and not judge me. Judgment belongs to Jesus, not man! As I wrote out my confession and prayer of forgiveness, open your hearts to understand why I was so open. My cries are not just about me they are for all single adults that are or want to be a Christian. I have prayed for single adults for over ten years. I know their needs! Somehow we need to open the doors to the churches for single adult ministries, why not! This would help the hurting bring in new families to the church, and add to the church. Single adults are near 50% of all adults. They need a church home. I'm asking the pastors and churches to open your doors to single adult ministries it's a real need. Don't judge single adult ministries. Just support them. You as a single adult should always bring this up to your church and pastor. It's a great ministry. You know the churches have all types of activities but for most they fail to have single adult's activities. Why is that? Single Adults need something to do to keep them within the walls of the church. By opening the church door to single adult ministry we may be closing the door to (bars, alcohol, drugs, loneliness, sex, homosexuality, the loss of homes, divorce, gambling, abortion, astrology, backsliding, the occult etc.) There is a lot of trouble that single adults can get themselves into, I know. So open the doors to the church, to help out with this single adult ministry, for it is the house of God.

<u>Matthew 7:1-2</u> *JUDGE not, that ye be not judged. Vs. 2: For with what judgment ye judge, ye shall be judged: and with what measure ye mete, it shall be measure ye mete, it shall be measured to you again.*

Let Jesus, clean us

If we stain the temple (our body) with sin, it will take time to clean the temple out. How do we clean the temple out that is our body? With confession, prayer, repenting, and rest in the Lord Jesus Christ. But more so, let Jesus Christ clean us from our sins. After confession and repentance of our sins, we must give thanks to Christ in thanksgivings. Thanksgivings will rebuild you and your relationship with God our Father. This will allow you to grow and become stronger in the Lord Jesus Christ. We must get back to the basics with God, be childlike in Christ. **We know when we sin; therefore we know when we need Jesus Christ, Amen! Remember, it will take Jesus to clean you from sin.** When you get past the hurt, ask God to send you a soul mate. **God wants his church to be full of families. That's how the church grows.** This will also cause unity in the church!
Your future depends on you and Jesus Christ everyday!
That is why we must find a way back to God our Father!
There are so many Bible verses about letting Jesus clean up our lives. So I'm going to share with you what a friend told me one day. I had gone through a broken relationship that involved sexual sin, and I was hurt beyond repair. **Sin can get to the point where you cannot help your- self. This is a fact that Christians need to understand. It takes Jesus Christ everyday of our life to overcome the flesh!** *My brother in Christ told me to go back and read the book of John. It took me a few weeks to understand what he was saying. But he was right. I was caught up in the flesh and took my eyes and heart off of God.*
READ THE BOOK OF JOHN!

Fantasy

Our imagination and fantasy will cause us to overlook what God has sent! **What if God has sent you your soul mate and you overlook them or just walk away?** *What would you do if God revealed this to you? Could or would you be strong enough to go back to that person and share with them the truth? Could you ask to fix what you broke? If you were approached by someone who did this, could you forgive? Could you accept the real truth?* **Leaving what God may have sent you because you were looking for greener grass is one of the greatest mistakes some of us have made!**

I ask that all of you that reads this part of this book to stop and pray about this. Ask God to show you the truth about your past relationships. (Father God, did I over look what you sent me?) *Could you be man or woman enough to go back and see if God and you can put this relationship back together? In truth and in peace!* Remember your prayers you said about this person that you were in a relationship with? Did you walk away?

If God is revealing something to you, what are you going to do? The grass is only green for a time. I know that some of us have walked away from what God had sent. I know it may take time to rebuild a past relationship. But if God had put two together you have a real chance! Be strong, of courage and try to get back with the one that God had sent.

Remember this, God can only bless if you would only receive! To those of you that were abandon. If your soul mate was to return, could you accept them back? This will be a real challenge for most of you. This is where it gets tough. **I would trade all the green grass of this world to lay with my soul mate in a soft place called marriage!**

Hebrews 11:6 *But without faith it is impossible to please him: For he that cometh to God must believe that he is, and that he is a rewarder of them that diligently seek him.*

John 12:37 *But though he (Jesus Christ) had done so many miracles before them, yet they believe not on him:*

Don't run to a relationship with a fantasy. It will end up in a real mess. Someone will be hurt in this type of relationship for most couples. ***Pray about this in FAITH***

Taking time to get over the hurt!

How long will it take to get over the hurt? It could take days, weeks, months and years. This is where I'm going to write in a prayer to set you free:

Father God, I come to you this hour to be released of this hurt and pain.
Father, this feeling is real and I need to believe in you only and not this fear, hurt, and pain!
Lord Jesus Chris, I pray that you would release this anxiety and grant me the peace I need!
Bring forth a new life and forgive me where I failed.
Father, help me grow in faith!
AMEN!

Your daily walk is one step at a time with Jesus Christ every day! You may have to fight to keep from looking back at the past! Just go back and read the prayer above when you're in pain about your broken relationship. It may take time and prayers to get you past the hurt. But you must keep praying in order to get past the hurt!

Psalm 34:15-17 *The eyes of the Lord are upon the righteous, and his ears are open unto their cry. Vs. 16: The face of the Lord against them that do evil, to cut off the remembrance of them from the earth. Vs. 17:* **The righteous cry, and the LORD heareth, and delivereth them out of all their troubles.**

This is what will help you get over a broken relationship. Make a list of small goals, with just a few long-term goals. This will give you something to work on and may take your mind off this past relationship. ***Remember, without a vision my people perish.*** If you want your life back have a vision! Set your goals with Jesus in your heart. *READ: Habakkuk 2:1-4 (The just shall live by faith). Write down your vision and make it plain!*

Time to forget and move on!

When love falls all apart, and you are still in love. I'm speaking from my heart; I really know how hard this can be. ***There is a hurt that can't be explained. Love hurts and that's the truth****. This is one of the hardest lessons of life that you may ever come to know.* Even when one knows what to do, this will still take some time to get over. It may seem that you're taking a few steps forward and a few steps backwards. You may come to the point where you feel God has left you. I know how that really feels. That's when one must keep praying and looking for the word of God (Bible). Seek God in all things and give God thanks in all things. That may be real hard for you to do. I know, I wrote this with a broken heart. In hopes that I may reach just one that will overcome this pain of a broken heart! This is where you must walk softly; the ground that you're walking on may feel like its sinking. This is where you don't need to look back. When you do look back, stop and pray. Even if tears fall, pray.
If you would pray yourself through the pain, there will come a day when you will run and laugh once again. Praise God!

Why does it take so long? Your love was real. Love can tear down the strongest man or woman. There may not be an answer to any of this pain. But the answer is in your own heart as you let God help you. Healing may come in small steps. It's just like walking all over again. May I suggest this to you? Just keep walking with God. If we walk with Jesus Christ, we will walk out of this pain.

Isaiah 26:3 *Thou wilt keep him in perfect peace, whose mind is stayed on thee: because he trusth in thee.*

Romans 8:28 *And we know that all things work together for good to them that love God, to them who are the called according to his purpose.*

Signs to look for
before you enter into another bad relationship

1: They want sex fast: *They do this for many reasons: they may be hurt; it's their way of life, to get back at someone else, feel a need to be with someone all night, use you as a fill in, they may not be able to be alone, they hurt and feel the need to have someone for a time so that they aren't alone, sex to them may be a way to say I love you or think they love you.*

2: Wants you to meet their family as soon as possible: *Just to show off what they have or have found. Look at what I got! They may do this to let the person that hurt them see I can get someone else. They may do this to get back into a past relationship!*

3: A taker: *You may find yourself buying things for them. A good person would tell you, you don't have to do this. I don't feel good about taking the things you are giving me. The taker will just keep taking until they find someone else or greener grass. Your gift may not mean anything to the taker. Your gift doesn't make love real in the takers life. They only use people. A taker is a thief and a liar! They will stay with you until they find greener grass.*

4: When someone is not trying to lead or make the relationship grow: *They are just using you to have fun. They are called fake lovers and this will cause someone to get really hurt. They are having sex to fill their desires.*

5: You are the one that creates the things to do: *The other person doesn't try to have activities from their part of the relationship. They are just there to enjoy themselves and use you. They will do this until they find greener grass! Look out for this type!*

6: Agrees to everything you want to do or what you say: *They do this, to have something to fall back on; so they can say: I'm tired of doing it your way. This is the scapegoat, and they were just there for a free ride!*

7: Their whole family may be in sin: *This creates a bad past for them to overcome. They may be only living for themselves. This may not always be true but for the most part it is! They will drag you down into their hell!*

8: Someone who can't make decisions: *This is a person that has no motivation in a relationship. Once again they are there just to have someone near them or just for fun. This type of adults are likely to spend time to use someone, again as a fill in type of relationship.*

Beware of this! _People, who don't know, are people who can cause the most hell!_

9: May want you to do things for them: _Like, fix things in their house, not share in expense, pay their bills, doing their laundry; they always have something for you to do. Remember a relationship isn't being a slave!_

Proverbs 27:6 _Faithful are the wounds of a friend; but the kisses of an enemy are deceitful._

Proverbs 17:17 _A friend loveth at all times...._

Leviticus 19:11 _Ye shall not steal, neither deal falsely, nether lie one to another._

Don't mess up someone's life

I want to hit the nail real hard here!
You and I don't have the right to mess up someone's life!

If you are using someone to fill-in your time because of your loneliness and desires, this is not of God at all. Always remember when you hurt someone that's a child of God. (This will be returned to you and your kind sooner or later, but it will happen in God's time). This is something I have done: Each time I meet someone that I had sex with or a bad relationship, I have asked them to forgive me for my action and fault. For the most part they are shocked and willing to forgive me. I then explained to them that I'm living for God, Jesus, and The Holy Spirit.

When we have sex outside of marriage, someone is set up to get hurt. That's a fact that you and every one can take to the bank! Why are 40 to 50 percent of adults single today in America?

1: No commitment.
2: No faith or real love
3: Don't give a care
4: Rejection
5: I can make it on my own
6: I can go out with whomever I want
7: No fear
8: No knowledge of a family life
9: Doesn't live like Christ
10: Any reason you can think of
(This is just a small list, what's yours)?
These are just a few facts, I am sure you and I can come up with a list as long as my arm!

But the real reason there is no commitment among the single adults. WHY? **_One other great reason is, they can't love or they are afraid to love!_** Why do single adults mislead one another to the point where someone is really hurt? *All the free sex you had in a relationship will not cover the pain or hurt that it will cause! To the one that is using or misleading someone, believe me when I say this: YOUR DAY IS COMING, AND IT'S WITH IN A SHORT DISTANCE OF GOD'S HANDS!* Then where will you stand?

What about those who think-having sex is love? You are foolish, and you don't know what love is truly about! Your day is coming. Believe me, what goes around comes around! If you're a fool you will be mixed up with fools!

Running from one relationship to another. Most people are always looking for green grass. This will only cause you to fall. Anything that is hot can burn you!

Proverbs 14:14 *The backslider in heart shall be filled with his own ways....*

Jeremiah 15:6 Thou hast forsaken me, saith the LORD, thou art gone backward; therefore I will stretch out my hand against thee, and destroy thee; I am weary with repenting.

Proverbs 17:20 *He that hath a forward heart findeth no good: and he that hath a perverse tongue falleth into mischief.*

Psalm 119:11 *Thy word have I hid in mine heart, that I might not sin against thee.*

James 4:7 *Submit yourselves therefore to God. Resist the devil, and he will flee from you.*

Have you walked away from what God may have sent you?

How many of us have done this?
This may be the 2nd chance you've been asking for. Does God give us a 2nd chance with someone? Yes! But we must take action in these steps. These steps are real hard! These steps are of respect and should be used as such! You should not chase a person. This may take some time to see what might happen. This is where one will have to take their time.
Let's look at the steps that one will have to overcome.
These are just a few and you will have to find the one's I leave out
to fit your needs of repair!

1: Ask God to forgive you for this mistake.
2: Be really aware that this person was for you as a soul mate!
3: Why did you leave this person?
4: How did you hurt this person?
5: Are you willing to tell the truth about this relationship you had with that person?
6: Are you willing to spend time in prayer and searching the Bible for the real answers?
7: Can you prove yourself to be true?

8: Can you become friends with this person?

9: What if this person has found another relationship?

10: Don't push yourself onto someone, if they aren't ready!

11: Can you talk about your sins?

12: Can you outline the type of relationship you want to have?

13: Are you willing to except rejection?

These are just a few questions you will have to answer

Let me ask you again, *did you walk away from what God has sent you?* **This is a big question.** If so, what are you going to do about this? How can you find the path back to the person that God had sent you? Are you willing to lay down your life for Christ? Believe me, this is what it might take. This may be the only way that the other person may see the truth in you! If you have hurt the other person or just used them; this will be real hard to do. But, if you have God on your side, you have a better chance. **God doesn't mess with the will of someone and neither should you!**

I want to share with all who read this. *If you know that you walked away from what God has sent, you may have a chance to recover this relationship in time.* **All things are possible with God!** So where do I go from here? Prayer! This is where you will need prayer time. Too find your inner self, and the truth of a past relationship. This will take a lot of time. This is also where you should send time reading the Bible. The other thing, I want to bring up is attend single adults ministries. This will help you to understand the needs of the other person in the broken relationship. Time is needed here as well.

It is better to try and fail than to never have tried. Step up to your mistakes. ***We need to get single adults to work toward marriage, not mistakes!*** *What if it doesn't work out? You have tried.* That may be the only blessing that may come out of your efforts. But that's a good thing and a God thing. Remember it may or may not work out. It's your mistake it's your effort and a time of forgiveness! Pray that God our Father will show you in your prayer time, maybe by visions, dreams, or by speaking to you audibly.

1John 1:9 *If we confess our sins, he is faithful and just to forgive us our sins, and to cleanse us from all unrighteousness.*

Matthew 10:32-33 *Whosoever therefore shall confess me before men, him will I confess also before my Father which is in heaven. Vs. 33: But whosoever shall deny me before men, him will I also deny before my Father which is in heaven.*

Psalm 32:5 *I Acknowledged my sin unto thee, and mine iniquity have I not hid. I said, I will confess my transgressions unto the LORD; and thou forgavest the iniquity of my sin Selah.*

Praying for your soul mate

This is prayer time in faith.

We as Christians should be praying for our soul mate everyday! ***Don't stop this prayer until you have been given your soul mate from God.*** What kind of soul mate do you want? God will need to know this. Write down what kind of soul mate you want. Write this out by faith and pray over the soul mate you want. You may need to make changes when you find the truth in prayer time. Place it in your Bible, and have faith in this. This may save a lot of hurt and time.

YOUR SOUL MATE IS WORTH PRAYING FOR EVERYDAY!

Hebrews 11:1
Now faith is the substance of things hoped for, the evidence of things not seen.

Write out your prayer, of the type of person you want as a soul mate. Do this on a piece of paper.
Or save this page and make a copy of this, to write.

_____
_____
_____
_____
_____
_____
_____
_____
_____
_____
_____
_____
_____
_____
_____
_____
_____
_____
_____
_____
_____

PART TWO

This part of the book was written, while I was working in support of our military in Iraq.
This part of the book is to help you get back into a relationship.
These two poems I wrote are written to make you think about the word Love and Friends.

Love

Little word with so much life.
Only you, I don't have to think twice.
Very real feelings about you.
Eve was made for Adam, so what do we do?

The above is to show you, loving you is fun.
I really believe you're the one.
I'm only asking for a commitment,
To allow our love to grow!
I'm committed to the time it takes,
So let's take it slow.
Committed to say these three words.
I LOVE YOU!

By: Bill Carter
12/26/06

FRIENDS

*F*riends are few and far between.

*R*eal friends are there even to the end.

I know you kept me in your prayers.

*E*very time I need help, you are always there.

*N*o one else could have made life this fun.

*D*oing everything we have under the sun.

*S*o what a friend I have in you.

Thanks for being just you!

By: Bill Carter
12/11/06

Relationship commitment

What does the word commitment mean to you and others? What has happed to this word in our real life relationships? Have we come to the point in our human life where the word commitment is just a disposable relationship? Does our commitment (now) include trading people to get what we want? People have been creating fake relationships for too long. Now they have false commitments just to please themselves. This is the reason for divorces, broken relationships, and this is why they have increase throughout the years. Let me prove this. *How many false relationships have you been in?* **Maybe, too many to count!**
People can't stay committed for more than a few months. What is going on with this? Let's take a look at this word.

Commitment: *to put into charge or trust: entrust, to pledge or assign to some particular course or use.*

But this generation of Men and Women can't keep their entrusted pledges. If this is the real problem, why are we allowing ourselves to be torn apart from relationship commitments? When you are in a relationship without commitments, you may well be wasting your time and setting yourself up to be hurt. You are investing your heart and time in the wrong person. This is a real foolish mistake.
You may be in a relationship where one would say, friends only! It's when two people touch or have sex that brings forth the hurt. So, since when has friendship hurt or used each other; friends are friends, read the poem I wrote.
So this generation doesn't live with real commitments, why? The Bible makes it so clear. The Bible states at the end times we would live like the days of Noah. We have accepted the ways of our sinful lust, to fill ourselves with sin. This is our choice and we have no one to blame.

One would ask is it just the People, Churches or Satan that has caused us to live without commitments?

Has the Church fallen away? The Church has not fallen away! But I feel they could do a better job in ministering to the single adults. The church needs to step up here and teach single adults who they are in Christ. The church needs to teach the real value of commitments and single adults that work toward marriage; not broken relationships or broken marriages. This is where we build families. Without families we have no church. The family supports the church. Being single in a church will allow a church to grow if we teach commitment toward marriage. Without commitments, we are messing with God's plans! This is why churches need to open their doors to single adult ministry. This will help keep the church alive and growing. ***Single adults are one of the signs of a growing church.***
Does Satan have a part in our lifestyle, (of no commitments)?
Only if you allow him! We have a God given right as Christians (child of God) to run Satan out of our relationships. I say that because we know what to expect from the Devil, and

what God has given us. Satan can only operate as much as you allow him to. You need to kick Satan out of your life. How can one do this? Don't open the door to temptation. If you do, you have allowed Satan and all of his fallen angels, to temp you and the one you're trying to have a relationship with. Sexual temptation has been the fall of mankind. *I want to state this; Satan does not have control over you if you are a child of God.* Yes, we have sin in our life from time to time. We are not perfect! That is why we should repent. Walk in the way of Christ. The influence and temptation that Satan has on this world is real. That is why we need to be a Christian and live a life of a Christian.

We need our men to be spiritual leaders and the women to be spiritual as well!

What about the flesh (man and women) factor?

Where is the real blame for this type of life style? Why are we having relationships without real commitments? It's not the Church! The temptation from Satan is just a little part of this, if you are a real Christian! What about Hollywood? No, it's not Hollywood either! *It's because we are not walking in the spirit of God.* **The truth is when man stopped being the spiritual leader and women stopped their spiritual walk with God; the relationships lost their commitments.** Mankind is the blame for this. This is why we don't have real commitments! *I've said this a thousand times and I'm going to say this again,* "**People who fall in love (short time) for the most will fall out of love. This was and is a fake relationship, without real commitments. People that grow in love (taking their time) have a real foundation of love. This is where we see real commitments**". We have a free well to be good or bad. To walk in sin or not to walk sin, **these choices are made on a human level! It's up to you!** Commitments should be real and kept. For this is the will of God our Father. In keeping your commitments God will bless you and reward you. Only foolish people break commitments. We all know what happens to foolish people. The Bible makes it real clear.

The truth is we should keep our commitments alive in the spirit of God!

When you want something you have never had.
You have got to do something you never done!

This is why we must live in a committed
Relationship!

John 13:17 *If ye know these things, happy are ye if ye do them.*

Friendship or love
Which is it?

Friendship comes from the word Friend. What is a friend?
1: one attached to another by respect or affection.
2: acquaintance
3: one who is not hostile.
4: one who supports or favors something.
5: a member of society of friends

Don't mistake friendship.
For someone who isn't worth having a long term relationship with!
Wisdom is needed here!

Love, what is love?
1: strong affection.
2: warm attachment.
3: attraction based on Godly sexual desires, (to be married).
4: a real beloved person
5: unselfish loyal and concern for others.

Love is worth a real commitment and a lifelong commitment.
True love is hard to find and must be kept alive
By your commitments, everyday!

I want to show you a true commitment, spoken by a woman.
If Ruth can speak this way from her heart,
Why can't man and woman.
Understand the power of commitment through real love and compassion?

<u>Ruth 1:16,17</u> *And Ruth said, Entreat me not to leave thee, or to return from following after thee: for whither thou goest, I will go; and where thou lodgest, I will lodge: thy people shall be my people, and thy God my God: Where thou diest, I will die, and there will I be buried: the LORD do so to me, and more also, if ought but death part thee and me.*

Have you felt this commitment in love?
Can you compare your love this way?

You are on trial for love

You have been asked to come to a court of law to prove your love that you have claimed.
You're in love with this other person; in your relationship. You have to represent you self.
For just a moment as you read this trial for love.
Take a mental image of this courtroom setting.
The judge happens to be the person you say you love.
The jury is people from your past relationships.
You are walking into the courtroom. Your friends, people from your church and a few of
your family members are sitting in this courtroom to give you support. As you walk in they
are looking at you with suspicion. Now as you walk to your seat you begin to wonder about
yourself and the outcome of this trial. You take your seat and it's only you and a glass of
water that will separate, you from the jury and the judge. You are hearing a few comments
in the background.

Then walk out the people who make up the jury (all of your Ex's). And they all look at you
one at a time. They are just as dumbfounded as you are. There is a still chill in this
courtroom as you wait for the judge to walk out. (By the way the judge didn't know he or
she would judge your case, nor did you). As the judge walks out to take a seat; the judge
gives you a smile and wonders what you going to say. Now remember it's up to the jury to
make the decision if you are telling the truth.

The judge reads why you're here, and the judge reads a statement that you must answer.
The judge has asked you to prove that you love this person in your relationship. You must
convince this jury and the judge. By writing out a detail outline of facts and reasons why you
have a real love for the other person involved. The judge asked that you do this with in
thirty minutes, and with less than 300 words. They hand you a pen a paper. Then the judge
asked you to start your writing.

Here is where I want you to write out why you love or have loved someone.
You may need more room for this, use a pad to write on.

_____

_____

_____

_____

_____

_____

_____

_____

_____

_____

_____

_____

_____

_____

_____

_____

_____

_____

_____

_____

_____

_____

_____

_____

_____

_____

_____

_____

_____

_____

_____

_____

_____

_____

_____

_____

_____

_____

_____

_____

Don't look at the next page;
until you have written out, why you are in love.
If you are not in love at this point in your life, write out why you have been in love before.

The judge has just walked back into the courtroom.
Everyone has taken their seat. The judge has given you time allowed. It is time to hand over the facts and reasons. The judge has asked that you read your statement to the jury and court.
(At this point I want you to go to your mirror and read your statement aloud).
<u>*Just play along, I'm trying to get you to understand real love.*</u>

You just completed your statement. How do you think the jury and judge took your statement?
Then a man walked into the courtroom. He begins to speak with wisdom, to inform the court and you. He reveals what real love is! The court and you sit back into your seats not knowing what to expect.

There is a sound of thunder as this strange man begins to speak.
"Real relationships need real commitments of love. That you will need to renew everyday of your life. There are three types of Love, (EROS, PHILIA and AGAPE). I'm here to tell you and this court the truth concerning love. Today I stand before you with the truth about LOVE"!

From the Webster's dictionary:

Eros: It's a Greek word: Sexual love, to love, desire
1: the Greek god of erotic love – *(this could be sexual without real love)*
2: The aggregate of life-preserving instincts that are manifested as impulses to gratify basic needs (as sex), sublimated impulses motivated by the same needs, and impulses serving to protect and preserve the body and mind.
3: often not cap: aspiring and fulfilling love often having a sensual quality: Desire, Yearning

Philia: It's a Greek word: friendship, Dear
1: Tendency toward (someone)
2: Abnormal appetite or liking for (it can all so mean (philic: having an affinity for: love (look at the word affinity: 1: kinship, relationship. 2: attractive force: attractive sympathy) .

Agape: It's a Greek word: love
1: Love feast
2: love – (this is real love)
3: The strongest kind of love

Let's look at a few more word out of the dictionary:

Love feast:
1: A meal eaten in common by a Christian congregation in token of brotherly love.
2: A gathering held to promote reconciliation, and good feelings. Or show someone affectionate honor.

Love:
1a: a strong affection for another arising out of kinship or personal ties
1b: attraction based on sexual desire: affection and tenderness felt by lovers.
1c: affection based on admiration, benevolence, or common interest – an assurance of love.
2:   warm attachment, enthusiasm, or devotion.
3:   the object of attachment, devotion or admiration.
3b: a beloved person, darling – often used as term of endearment.
4: unselfish loyal and benevolent concern for the good of another.

Love affair:
1: a romantic attachment or episode between lovers.
2: a lively enthusiasm.

Relationship:
1: a romantic or passionate attachment.

Marriage:
1: The institution, where by men and women are joined in special kind of social and legal dependence, for the purpose of founding and maintaining a family.
1b: the rite by which the married status is affected.

After you had read your statement aloud to the courtroom. How does it match up to what the stranger said? Did the jury and judge accept your statement as the truth? Have you been in any fake relationships? Did you have a real idea of love? Do you have the truth of love now?

Now let's look at these three words (Eros, Philia and Agape) from a Christian point of view.

Eros: It is inspired by the biological structure of human nature (man and woman). The husband and wife, in a good marriage, will love each other romantically and erotically, forever! Eros is the love, sexual love. This type of love should be handled in a Christian way. (In marriage)!

Philia: In a good marriage the husband and wife are also friends. It's a best friend relationship. This type of friendship means companionship, communication and cooperation. (Everyday)! Philia is family love. This is where brotherly love comes from.

Agape: Unconditional love, self-giving love, gift of love, the love that goes on loving. Even when love, becomes unlovable. I believe Agape love is not just something that happens to you; it's something you make happen. This is a gift of love. God Himself showed this unconditional love. We share this love by faith and by His spirit. Agape love will grow in a real relationship and marriage. That's why we should grow in love, not fall in love!

If people, would take these three words, (Eros, Philia and Agape).
Make them into a three cord rope, to make their love stronger.
Their love would last a lifetime!
If companions would only, put forth efforts purposely to increase, Philia and Agape love, this alone would increase their Eros love. This is when Eros love will flourish if properly nurtured. If people, would increase in the area of Eros love. This will reinforce the Philia and Agape love. Now you see why the three strand cord of love will last a lifetime in a marriage! These three types of love will keep and save your companionship!

Love will die when you spend little or no time together, or when you stop sharing actives that are mutually enjoyed; (remember this)! Love is created or destroyed if there is or isn't pleasurable actives over a period of time. So stay involved by interacting with each other. Don't let your love die. This is your responsibility! **If couples don't reinforce their love, it will just die.**

Real love requires the ability to put yourself in your companion's place. So you would understand the differences of two very unique personalities. Rather than betrayals you would have in faith, hope and love, the true love of companionship, and the unconditional willingness of each of you (man and woman) to keep your love alive. To understand and resolve these differences through the sharing of your deepest feelings, concerns, attitudes and ideals. Is a fundamental component of real love, companionship and marriage!

Now, did you know what love was about?
If everyone, could write their statement of love like this.
I believe their love, would be a love for a lifetime!

Proverbs 18:22
Whoso findeth a wife findeth a good thing, and obtaineth favor of the LORD.
Hebrews 13:4
Marriage is honourable in all, and the bed undefiled:

Give to another, what he or she cannot find anywhere else.
And he or she will keep returning!
One way to do this is to grow into companionship love.

Love for a reason, forever

I will say this until the day I can no longer speak. **When we grow in love, we should be building a foundation of love.** *This will cause love to live and last in your relationship. Love for a reason, forever!*

I want to share with you that the three strand rope of love is strong, (Eros, Philia and Agape). When or where does love die in a relationship? If you let one of these three die, Eros, Philia, or Agape. Then love may die.

Eros, Philia and Agape are the complete foundation of love. Without one of these three parts of love; love will fall apart! **How do we break the three cords of love? Negative activites!** The more negative your action is, the less your love grows. If love stops growing, love will start dieing.

Love must be nurtured and reinforced. Each companion must work on relationship issues, to keep love alive. We must say and show love, every day and every night! Love for a reason, forever!

People love for a reason. What reason, forever!

We need to correct our mistake as single adults
And
Work toward Marriages

FOREVER

Found real love with you

Oneness is the greatest of all love

Rather have and be with you

Each day I pray that God would keep and bless us

Very important to say I love you, daily

Even today, I think you are still the one for me

Rest of my life, with you only

By: Bill Carter 4/24/07

Love can and will change People!

Hebrew 10-36
For ye have need of patience,
that,
after ye have done the will of God,
ye might receive the promise.

Love can and will change people. Love will bring forth the growth in one's life. If love can forgive sin; then love can forgive, heals, bless and teach. *So if love can do these things, why don't we let love grow in our relationship building?* If love could change you to become a better person would you allow love to be a teacher! Would you change to keep your relationship alive?

Love also gives, but you need to give as well. Can you be a giver in your relationship? Would you care enough to keep your heart warm toward your partner? That's what a giver can give, that how love can and will change people.

I will only spend a little time here on this subject.

BAD HABITS

If you know you have a bad habit or habits. Change them as soon as possible. No one needs to ask you to do this! *This brings forth a giving type of love.* If a companion, asks you to change, realize it may be for the best. But each companion needs to realize, change takes time. One may even need to learn how to change. **Remember if we allow love to be a teacher, your relationship will not only grow, but become stronger.**

Forgiving is a must in all parts of your companionship. In order to be forgiven you must forgive.

Forgiving is a part of teaching in your relationship growth. If you can't forgive sooner, or later you are not going to trust. When you don't forgive you are judging. The Bible is clear on this issue.

(Don't judge lest you be judged).

There may or will be times when we hurt our companion's feelings. This is where he and she must learn to heal and give healing. **Saying "I'm sorry" is very hard for many people, especially those who have been hurt in a past relationship.** As I have grown, it's not hard for me to say "I'm sorry for my action". You don't need to repeat your wrong actions; only grow from your mistakes. This will allow love to grow and become stronger.

Let me ask you to do something. Write out the things in your life that you need to change. We all have things we can change. Is having a loving relationship, worth changing for? I believe so, and I'm sure you believe so! So take the time to write out the changes that you should make in your life.

Changes I need to make in my life.

_____

_____

_____

_____

_____

_____

_____

_____

_____

_____

_____

_____

_____

_____

_____

_____

_____

_____

_____

_____

_____

_____

_____

_____

_____

_____

_____

I hope you took the time to list a few changes you really need to make in your life.
Now I would like you to ask God in the name of Jesus Christ,
to help you make these changes.
Please pray about these changes!
Remember changes take time.
Just keep praying.
LOVE CAN AND WILL CHANGE PEOPLE!

Change

Chance to see something new in my life

Having the opportunity to learn

A new day to adapt

Never say no until you really try

Give it a real chance

Everyone is subject to change

By: Bill Carter
4/25/07

Future

Future

Finding a better path in life to take

Unfinished walk in one's life

The reason for living a greater life

Utilizing my past resources

Rather be me than anyone else

Even my failures make me a better person

By: Bill Carter
4/25/07

It's your future; it's up to you to choose your path that you will walk. So you have a chance to utilize your past resources. In knowing this, take a moment and write out a few goals for a relationship you would want to have. *In order to have something, you must know what you want.*

_____

_____

_____

_____

_____

_____

Imagination relationships

Don't allow yourself to be a part of this deceiving relationship. If you are living in an imagination life style, that's a bad habit! A person that's in ***imaginary relationship;*** they fall in love, versus growing in love. ***Imagination is something not present to senses or not previously known or experienced by people. Their creative ability is not reality.*** They just image love in a relationship and this is a false love! As you grow toward love and a relationship; you must change your bad habits.

Here an example of Imagination / Relation

Two people meet, they go out they touch, kiss or have sex. (Sex is not love at this point.) After this point one of them will say I'm in love, they will do this within a few days to less than 14 days. This is far from the truth! **It takes time to trust someone; without trust how can you love?** *They have only allowed their imagination to take over their emotions. They are not in control of their reality! They may not even know this.* **This is why I give great caution about people that fall in love quickly.** *Stay away from this type of relationship. They will only say they love you.*

Until their imagination tells them that they love someone else. ***This is one of many types of false relationship! Just because someone said they love you, does not mean they really do. Love is a word that is often mess used! Ask that person who had said they love you why and how they love you. If they say, I don't know I just love you; this is not love! This is a warning give to those who seek a long term relationship that leads to marriage!***

One must build trust in order to love.
If your trust doesn't grow, where is the love?
Don't allow yourself to be pulled into a false relationship.
How can we avoid this?

Ask the person you're trying to date, about their wants in a relationship. **Open that person mind and look at their imagination and reality.** When they speak about these issues of; controlling, domination, ruling, fear, consuming your time, and how much attention they really need or want. Be very cautious here, if they have pointed out these issues without reality of a real relationship; it may be best to avoid this relationship.

People in a real relationship; will build goals together! This is a working relationship!
I'm here to tell you, that great relationship comes with a lot of quality work and time. You can count on this! Time is a part of relationship's foundation! In fake relationship, a person will try to place a title on you quickly. Remember you are not a title.

1 Corinthians 10:13
There hath no temptation taken you but such as is common to man (woman):
but God is faithful, who will not suffer you to be tempted above that ye are
able; but will with the temptation also make a way to escape,
that ye may be able to bear it.

This one verse will protect you, all the days of your life.
If you would learn to use this verse!
So what does one do to keep them self out of an
Imaginary Relationships?

1: Ask them about their dream relationship?
2: Ask them how many relationship or marriages they have been in?
3: Ask them why they got a divorce, and each time they got divorce?
4: Ask them about all past relationships; see if they will give details?
5: Ask them how many people they had sex with in the past few years?
6: Ask them if they set goals in relationships? What can of goals do they have?
7: Ask them what type of person are they looking for?
8: Ask them if they are looking for a long term relationship?
9: How do they treat their family members and friends?
10: Then ask your self is this the person for me?

You owe it to yourself to ask these ten questions. When you ask these ten questions, go back at a later date and re asks these questions. See if they change their story, find out why. Get as much information about someone before you grow in love.

The truth is in the eyes. Please remember this!
Don't become a part of an imaginary relationship.
They will only drag you down.
So be wear!

James 1:12
Blessed is the man (or woman) that endureth temptation:
for when he is tried,
he (or she) shall receive the crown of life,
which the Lord hath promised to them that love him.

What you are willing to walk away from.
Will determine what God will bring into your life!

So involved, you don't see the truth

It all starts with finding someone you have chosen to go out with. So the first dates are ok to great. Maybe you and the other person become attractive to each other. Now, that these new feelings are fitting together. Then the two of you become more involved. You start doing the little things for each other. You two are doing these things because it makes you feel good.

This is where we become, *so involved you don't see the truth.* When we do these little things and they turn into bigger things. The little things that make you feel good. And the bigger things will make you feel great. During this time you're not putting a check on the real issue like the truth. I don't want you to be suspicious of everyone you date, but I do want you to be aware. **You don't want to put your heart in front of the truth.** You must trust before you grow in love. **Build a trust base on truth not feelings!**

When you are in the first stages of a relationship, take your time. Good feelings can be one sided. See if the other person can make you feel good. Allow a relationship to grow before you start loving. One must hold on to their heart, to know the truth.

Trust should come before love!

Proverbs 3:5-6
Trust in the LORD with all thine heart;
And lean not unto thine own understanding.
In all thy ways acknowledge him (the LORD),
And he (the LORD) shall direct thy paths.

Matthew 26: 41
Watch and pray, that ye enter not into temptation:
The spirit indeed is willing,
but the flesh is weak.

Love on the Job

Relationships on the job, love on the job or sex from a coworker. We all know this can spell trouble from the start. But in a few cases it can lead to be marriage. I read a few surveys about work force relationships. I made an average of these surveys and came up with this info:

- 43 percent of Americans have dated a co-worker
- 20 percent of those end up marrying the co-worker
- 10 percent say they currently having their eye on a co-worker that they would like to date.
- 35 percent of employees who have date a co-worker, said they had to keep their relationship, romance or sexual affairs a secret.
- 25 percent dated a higher-up.
- 22 percent sneaked around with a co-worker who was already married.
- 15 percent have had romance or sex with their boss.
- 11 percent had some type of romance or sex during lunch.
- 10 percent got together during happy hour.
- 15 percent made moves on each other while working late hours at the office or job.

This type of survey will vary, depending on which survey you read.

Having a relationship on the job can be a real risk. You must use a lot of caution here to avoid trouble. I want to point out something here in this survey. We have a high percentage of co-workers having sex with people that are already married. How many of them are Christian? A lot! I know that single adults have a hard time meeting someone who is right for them. But don't have an affair with someone who is married!

If you are single find a place where you can meet singles. A lot of Churches have single adults support or activities. Call some of the local Churches to find out if they have a singles department. Ask about the age group as well. Churches should be supporting single adult's activities. This is where we get our new families.

When you change your focus
You will change your future
So focus on true love
The house of God is full of love
Single adults, need to take their mistakes
And work toward marriage
You can't change your future
Until you change your focus

Part Three

This part of the book is to help us understand the mistakes we make.
And things we can change to help our relationship last.

Mistakes

May your mistakes be few in life!

I care about my mistakes and who they effect.

Sure need to admit my mistakes.

That's what makes me learn and grow maturity.

At least I'm stating the truth.

Keep focus on a great life.

Everyone can improve

So do your best

By: Bill Carter
4/29/07

Mistakes

I have made mistakes in the past! Most likely I will make a few in the future! *But if I don't admit my mistakes, I'll always be a mess. That's why I should be truthful about my mistakes.*

There are two great things that can come out of mistakes. You have an opportunity to learn, and mature as an adult. Can you turn your mistakes, into tools? That will teach you to develop quality skills as a person? Will your mistakes mature you? *We must grow, learn and let it show!*

When we admit our mistakes we are growing. This is where we start to learn. When we learn it should show.

In relationship growth, if we don't acknowledge our mistakes it can or will hurt your relationship. This is why we must be truthful. "Hey I made a mistake." If we state the truth, we might save our relationship from hurt and break up.

So remember that you are not perfect either.
Wisdom comes with time and mistakes.
Only if we are truthful!

Proverbs 3:13
Happy is a man (or woman) that findeth wisdom,
And the man (or woman) that getteth understanding.

Changing for a better relationship

A great relationship is worth any and all changes. That comes from either companion. To have a real loving and caring relationship you must grow. To grow means change; changes are needed in a real loving and caring relationship. Companions shouldn't have to be asked to change. Again changes take time. If your partner points out something, take a notice of what they said. It does take a lot of effort to change. *I agree, that one must be able to change them self.* Let your companion change them self. This will make the relationship stronger.

If you are not willing to change, why have a relationship?

Time is a real factor when it comes to new changes. Two people (companions) must realize that they will have real differences. This is true about all relationship. This rule applies to all new companions. Your relationship is worth all the work it takes to keep a relationship alive. Work through your differences, then watch love grow, to last a lifetime!

Changing for a greater relationship starts with you!
If you are dating someone who lives by this next statement;
"It's my way or the high way"! Get rid of them!

You don't want someone who isn't willing to change to make the relationship greater. You don't need a relationship with someone who talks foolishly. Don't waste your time! When a person will not change for the better of a relationship, just move on and find a greater person! Believe me, there are single adults looking to find a loving companion!

Remember, that change, is not about what's right or wrong.
It's about what is right, in creating a great team or companionship!
It's also about you as a team mate or a companion!

Rewards in one's life
Are determined
By the problems they solve

Proverbs 1:5
A wise man (or woman) will hear, and will increase learning;
and a man (or woman) of understanding
shall attain unto wise counsels.

Easily offended

Proverbs 11:14
Where no counsel is, the people fall:
But in the multitude of counsellers
There is safety.

Let's look at the word offend to see its roots.
Offend: *sin, transgress, to cause discomfort or pain, hurt, to cause dislike or vexation, annoy.*

It's in these areas that we get offended. We can get offended because of a bad day. We can get offended from misunderstanding. The way we speak can offend. Our level of people skills can offend. The way we handle our differences can cause a person to become offended. The way we treat people can cause one to be offended. *The willingness to change the mistakes one makes will not offend someone.* I can write pages on how we get offended. **But I want you to think about all the ways you offend people.** When we know we are offending someone, we should stop this action. If you make a mistake, admit it. When we offend someone accidentally, without intent or through carelessness, just give them time to understand what caused this discomfort. We don't always need to say I'm sorry. But it's a great thing to say, "I'm sorry and I care enough to say this"!

Remember you cannot change the truth!
If you offend someone address it, but be nicely detailed.
If someone offends you address it, but be nicely detailed.
The truth does two things.
It will inform and change people, if we allow it to.
The truth will set you free.

So I'm asking you to stop offending people.
Never call someone a name, or degrade anyone.
When we really love one another,
you should never offend anyone you love!
There shouldn't be any transgressions in a real relationship.
You have to trust and have peace, to love someone!

Controlling your tongue

Proverbs 8:13
The fear of the Lord is to hate evil:
pride, and arrogancy, and the evil way,
and the forward mouth, do I (GOD) hate.

Arrogant: offensively exaggerating one's own importance.
God hates a forward tongue. What more can I write about this issue? But yet, we do it every day. Somewhere, someday, somehow, we all need to learn to control our tongue. Controlling one's tongue is something we learn and have to practice. This generation of people has lost touch with this issue. But I will assure you if you don't control your tongue, life for you will be tough. The Bible makes it real clear, to safe guard your tongue.
You know as well as I do, that we must have great speaking skills in all relationships. When you speak with an evil tongue, you are condemning yourself! When you are not speaking with kindness you are dismantling the foundation of your relationship.
If you know you are harming a relationship by not controlling your tongue, why would someone have to ask you, to stop speaking in a way that you know offends people?

A word of warning! Don't fall in love with someone, who is out of control with their own tongue. *Most people, who aren't in control of their tongue, may not be fully in control of their mind either!* These types of people often speak without reason, they just make noise! Don't get mixed up with someone like this!

Proverbs 10:11
The mouth of a righteous man (or woman) is a well of life:
But violence covereth the mouth of the wicked.
(Read chapter six of Proverbs.)
Proverbs 6:16,19
These six things doth the Lord hate: yea, seven are an abomination
unto him (the Lord)

A false witness that speaketh lies, and he that soweth discord among
brethren (or loved ones).

*I want to invite you to read **James 3:1-12**, to get a full understanding of this passage!*

Conflict in your relationship

Let's look at the word conflict:

1: fight, battle, war

2a: competitive or opposing action of incompatibles: antagonistic (*hostile*) state or action (as of divergent ideas, interest or persons)

2b: mental struggle resulting from incompatible or opposing needs, drives, wishes, or external demands

3: the opposition of person or forces that gives rise to the dramatic in a drama or fiction

Note: conflict is discord

In your love life and relationship there will be conflicts. Each of us has our own desires, wants, needs, and goals. It's when any of these change from what we want or had in mind. That's when a conflict may occur. If we know why conflicts occur, **how do we stop these conflicts in relationship behaviors? There is only one answer, Love!**

Proverbs 10:12
Hatred stirreth up strifes:
But love covereth all sins.

We are human beings with our imperfections. That's why our beliefs, ideas, attitudes, feelings and behaviors are so different. It isn't the differences that make a problem, but it's how we react to the problem. It is how we act or overreact that will cause our problems. This is how conflicts start. It's how we handle our reactions that will limit or cause us to have unwanted behaviors in our conflict time.

Anger comes from; fear, hurt, and frustration! Before you have another conflict what area are you in; fear, hurt or frustration? Which is it? Don't allow yourself to enter in to, fear, hurt, or frustration. Conflict is a part of life. It is a real natural part of growth in friendships, families and relationships.

*Disagreements or conflicts don't always need to be resolved. Maybe time will change things. Or the person will change because of knowledge, wisdom, experience, or love. **This is growth change and is one of best changes we can make.***

I'm writing this because most people do not handle or deal openly with conflicts. Most of these issue forms around knowledge. *People don't understand effective ways of dealing with their conflicts. We should only allow the positive side of conflict to exist.* And give yourself the opportunity to grow in your personal life and relationships; with the understanding and knowledge of conflicts. It's up to you to do this. **Be committed to understand your conflicts!**

Conflict resolution

The greatest choice we have is to yield when we are having a conflict!

But it's how you handle the conflict. There are at least five things you can do that may bring conflicts to an end.

- *Knowledge*: One must be taught how to deal with conflicts. This may take time. Teaching someone who doesn't want to listen is hard. Teaching someone that wants to learn is rewarding. The real question is. "Do you want to live with conflicts?" Most people don't! So we must learn to change in relationship behaviors. *Don't allow your differences to become disagreements that will form into conflicts. If we learn this, we are ahead of the game.*

- *Withdrawing:* One can do this psychologically or physically. *(But for the most this doesn't bring any changes.)* This could cause you to feel incapable, and a loss of personal growth. This will not allow your relationship to grow. When couples do this, they bring more harm and hurt to the relationship. *The relationship will more likely end!*

- *Compromising:* A lot of companions do this. *Give a little take a little.* Compromising can work. *But your relationship may stay at the same level, and so will your love for each other.* Compromising is about giving and taking (but not in an uncaring and ungodly way). Love should give and build. Love isn't about taking or tearing down. When we give we are caring. **This type of compromising will work in your relationship. As long as both companions are givers and not takers.**

- *Resolving:* Conflicts should be about (situation, attitude and good behaviors). This can be changed by open and direct communication, that is given in love and understanding. If something really needs to be resolved in your relationship. Both companions should be listeners. Love can heal all things and forgive all things. If companions would only commit to each other. Respect plays a big part here. Remember you don't have to resolve every issue on the spot. Issues may take time. If you really love one another, time is a friend to relationship growth. In resolving your issues make sure it's fair for both companions.

- *Winning:* **Conflicts in a loving relationship is not about winning!** If you always want to win in your relationship conflicts, you are just dominating. Relationships will not grow in this environment. Do you want to win or have a loving relationship?

Relationships are always moving.
Either toward your goals,
Are away from them!

Reconciling
One word with a lot of life!

Reconcile:
1: settle, resolve
2: to make consistent
3: to cause to submit to or accept something unpleasant

There is a gift of love in this word, reconcile. In all relationships we must learn to reconcile. If we can't, what good is a relationship? In every relationship there or two unique people in a companionship, they have differences and similarities. Here are a few questions you must deal with in all relationships.
- How do you learn to adjust to the differences, your companion may have formed?
- Can you have a relationship, or have a marriage to a companion, that is unique?
- Can you learn to live with this person who is so different from you?

People need to answer these few questions before they start a relationship or even marriage. This is where two people need faith, trust and love. This is what will happen to the differences we have in each other. First they will attract. Then irritate, then frustrate, and finally unite them- selves in companionship. If they can reconcile! If there is no reconciliation there is no life in the relationship!

Love is worth reconciling.
Relationships are worth reconciling.
Marriages are worth reconciling.
Love is a real blessing.
It's hard to find a companion for a lifelong relationship.
Love is the greatest union of all.
If love grows, marriage will come.

Our expectations of people

In this part of our thinking this is where we get ourselves into trouble; with our imagination, disappointments, anger and lack of wisdom. Let's say you meet someone who you want to spend time with. You may have already set your expectation level of what this person or this relationship could be. This is where you will become disappointed. This will also cause you to stop growing in your relationship. That's like saying, "I fell in love with a one sided vision!" **When people set their expectation from the beginning or too early in the relationship; they are setting up their relationship for failure.** As love grows so does the relationship. *We must learn to allow the relationship to grow before we have any expectation!*

Before you have any expectation, allow yourself some time, in just having fun as you come to know the other person. Companionship comes with time. You must become friends first in all relationships. You must get past the attraction part as well. You should allow love to start to grow, (like in three months or so)! Then talk together about the real expectation of a relationship as companions. This will allow your love to grow on the foundation of companionship.

Write out some of your mistakes that you made with your expectation.

_____

_____

_____

_____

_____

_____

_____

_____

_____

_____

_____

_____

_____

_____

_____

_____

_____

_____

Communication in marriage and relationships

Three principles that need to be consistent to make communication in marriages and relationships complete:

1: You must be an **effective listener and speaker**. Don't make a mountain out of a molehill! Let the other person know your pay attention. One does not talk while he / she, is listening to their partner or spouse.

2: We must be able to **resolve conflicts through constructive methods.** To resolve conflicts, we can do this by **forgiveness, prayer, seeking peace, joy, and happiness.** You got married to live in love, peace, and joy. Keep this as a goal for a great marriage! *You can use this in your relationships as well.*

3: You must spend time on a daily basis in an **intimate sharing of feelings.** We must *learn* and become a *great listener*. When we share our feelings, **changes that are need and correction of simple misunderstandings will often be revealed.** *Remember that Marriage takes two to make one*, so why fight with one another! **After you have heard someone's feelings, why don't you spend some time with what they said!** *You can do this in your daily relationship*s *as well.*

What is Communication?

Most of the time when someone is talking, we believe that someone is listening! But, that's not always the case. *It takes two to communicate in a relationship!* It's a two way street in conversation, the giving and receiving of information. **(This involves more than talking.)** In communicating, we must have three things happening at once. What are the three things that are needed to have communication? **(Speaking, receiving and listening!)** The receiving and listening is a must, for communication to take place. It's just not speaking; this is a process that takes at least two people.
If we are able to do the first **three parts of** communication: **speaking, receiving and listening**
(or sharing of feelings). Look at what happens when we add **understanding.** We as people think that the other person has *understood,* what was said. That may not be the case. *So we need to explain our self with detail*. Don't expect someone to understand what you have said, if you can't explain what you're talking about. *In communication we need to have a speaker that can explain and listeners that receive and understand.*

Levels of communication

1: _**Small talk:**_ **This type of conversation, borders on meaningless communication. But small talk is a very important part of communication!** This is still better than the embarrassing silence. _**We should use small talk to break the ice, and start a conversation!**_

2: _**Facts in our communication:**_ This is where receiving or listening comes into play. "Listening" to facts will help your communication skills. So that is why we must speak in facts, stick to the facts. Don't add anything, stay on the facts. Communicate about what is; _**(reveal the facts.)**_ **We must learn not to add our feelings,** in the fact part of communication. _**(Yes this can be hard to do, but if we could learn to do this. Our communication skills would be greater.)**_
Men are more apt to settle for this level (for the most), than women. Men are less able to express their feelings. _Men focus more on the facts; while women focus on the feeling (or emotion with facts.)_

3: _**Ideas (thoughts), Feelings and Opinions:**_ **Intimacy begins here**. Why? When someone risks exposing his or her thoughts, feelings, and opinions in faith; they are trying to change or make better; themselves or issues. This is when we need to be a real listener. When you express yourself verbally, you have just verbalized your personal ideas, feelings, thoughts and opinions. _**This gives the person listening, a chance to know you better on an intimate level.**_

4: _**Emotion and Feelings:**_
This type of communication describes **what is going on inside of you.** This is how you feel about your partner, people or a situation. _**(This is when we verbalize feelings of anger, frustration, resentment, joy, love, happiness and peace.)**_
This is when we honestly share our interest in a speaking and listening behavior. _Make sure you show your interest in the other person's feelings._ This is where you can express your own feels. This will enrich and enlarge your relationship; _**(if you keep yourself humble!)**_ _If we would only learn to do this right;_ we could feel worthy, noticed, loved, appreciated and safe in our partner and friends affections. This will give you and the people around you an insight into you and your personality. This will give you a real understanding of how others think, or how others feel.

5: **A Deeper Insight:** _**This is when you are perfectly in tune with one another, in understanding, depth and emotional fulfillment.**_ Communication about such experiences often makes a deeper impression on both parties and this will enrich the relationship. _**Sharing of personal ideas and feeling is the ultimate goal in marital or relationship communication skills.**_ **Most marriages and relationships need deeper communication skills to keep their companionship growing!**

Effective speaking rules

1: Choose the right time to communicate with your spouse or companion
2: Develop a pleasant tone of voice
3: Be clear and specific
4: Be positive
5: Be courteous and respectful of your spouse or friends
6: Be sensitive to the needs and feelings of your spouse or friends
7: Develop the art of conversation

Rules for effective listening

1: Maintain good eye contact
2: Sit attentively
3: Act interested in what you are about to hear
4: Sprinkle your attentive listening with appropriate phrases to show agreement, interest and understanding
5: Ask well phrased, questions
6: Listen a little longer

Solving conflicts

1: Choose the best time and place
2: Say it straight, state your feelings openly
3: Stay on the subject; stick with one problem until you finish talking about the issue
4: Show respect, even when you don't agree
5: List the solutions
6: Evaluate the solutions
7: Choose the most acceptable solution
8: Decision, decide who is to do what, when and where

Keeping your marriage and relationship alive

1: Above all things, pray for one another
2: Forgive, as you have been forgiven
3: Speak and listen well
4: Remember why you are married and having a relationship
5: Find the solution or solutions
6: Talk every day about your feelings
7: Keep a regular Bible study
8: Last but not least, go to church often

Hebrews 11:1 *Now faith is the substance of things hoped for, the evidence of things not seen.*

We must watch our thoughts, for they become our words!
We must choose our words, for they become our actions!
We must understand our action, for they become our habits!
You must know your habits, for they become our character!
You must develop your character; one's character will affect your future!

By: EVANGELIST BILL CARTER
11/10/02

How can I improve my communication skills:

_____
_____
_____
_____
_____
_____
_____
_____
_____
_____
_____
_____
_____
_____
_____
_____
_____
_____
_____
_____
_____
_____

Arguing

Argue:

1: To exchange views about something in order to arrive at the truth or convinces others.

2: To contend in words.

3: To give evidence of or serve as ground for a valid or reasonable inference.

4: To uphold as true, right and proper, or acceptable often in the face of challenge or indifference.

If we argue, *we must learn how to arrive at the truth.* We can do this with *peace*! If we argue without *peace*, **"no one will listen!"**

The Bible states; "the truth shall set you free." In order to be set free, you must have *peace.* The truth will either set you free, or cause you to have problems with the way you think or the way you are! **Listening and arguing** goes hand in hand. In order to arrive at the truth we must listen to the argument. When one argues without a listener, we have no foundation for the truth to stand on.

Proverbs 15:31,32 *The ear that heareth the repoof of life abideth among the wise. vs 32: He that refuseth instruction despiseth his own soul: but he that heareth reproof getteth understanding.*

If we become offended with someone's argument; we must consider what the argument is about. When something needs to be confronted, or when something that needs to be changed, the truth needs to be found. If it's something that can't be fixed, seek the truth. But, keep in mind we all must forgive each other.

Hebrew 8:12 *For I will be merciful to their unrighteousness, and their sins and their iniquities will I remember no more.*

Ephesians 4:32 *And be ye kind one to another, tenderhearted, forgiving one another, even as God for Christ's sake hath forgiven you.*

WHAT GOOD IS ARGUMENT, IF WE HAVEN'T LEARNED HOW TO ARGUE?

Evangelist Bill Carter 6/29/02

How can I improve my arguing?

_____

_____

_____

_____

_____

_____

_____

_____

Never love anyone more than God

If we as single adults would only do what this title stated; this alone may keep us from getting into the wrong relationship, or getting hurt. **My pastor and brother Dr. Ed Davis told me right after a broken relationship.** That left me with a broken heart. *He said, "Bill never love someone more than God our Father, never."* Sin will keep you from God. Sin is sin; this will make division between God and mankind! That's a fact you can bank on. **Dr. Davis was right and let me show you why!**

<u>1John 4:19</u> *We love him (God our Father), because he first loved us.*

This is our first love. This is the love that heals; the love that hurts!
LOVE THAT HURT = that person wasn't a friend / mistakes / hate / broken relationship / bad relationship / Satan / sin
LOVE THAT HEALS = friend / love / forgiveness / understanding / peace / God our Father

It's when we take our eyes off God our Father; that will cause us to have a great fall in the flesh! Look up this Bible verse:
<u>1 John 5:7</u> *For there are three that bear record in heaven, the Father (God), the word (Jesus Christ), and the Holy Ghost (HOLY SPIRIT); and these three are one.*

When we keep our heart and eyes on God our Father, we have our first love. That is the greatest love known to mankind! I will speak openly here. *Marriage is a great thing in the eyes of God our Father. Marriage is where two people become one in Covenant.* **That is the love we as single adults should work toward, not mistakes!**
For the sake of knowing about love read:
1 John / 2 John / 3 John, These are small book and easy to understand. These short books will teach single adults a lot!

What happens when we take our heart and eyes off of God our Father? Flesh takes over!
FLESH = CARNAL
CARNAL: (Worldly), to give into the desires of the flesh; following their natural desires that leads the Christians into mistakes and sin.

What would happen if we would live by the Ten Commandments? *I will speak for myself. I would not be as carnal so* **what would happen to you if you kept the Ten Commandments? What is love? We know that it is about God being our first love. What is love? Let's turn to the next Bible verse:**

<u>2 John 2:4</u> *And this is love, that we walk after his commandments. This is the commandment. That, as ye have heard from the beginning, ye should walk in it.*

This is such a large verse. Let's look at this verse in parts: **1st part:** (and this is love), go back to **2 John 2:4 … we have received a commandment from the Father (God).** What was the commandment from God? We can find that answer in Exodus 20: 1-17 (The Ten Commandments). But let's look at **Exodus20: 1 *And God spake all these words saying. (God spoke these Ten Commandments)!* 2nd part:** That we walk after his commandments. (What are we doing if we are walking toward his commandments)? We are walking in his love not ours! If we walk after his commandments it is a narrow road. Look at the book of Matthew

Mathew 7: 13-14 *Enter ye in at the strait gate: for wide is the gate, and broad is the way, that leadeth to destruction, and many there be which go in thereat: Vs. 14: Because strait is the gate, and narrow is the way, which leadeth unto life, and few there be that find it.*

3rd part: That, as ye have heard from the beginning, ye should walk in it. (God spoke all these words saying).

John 14:15 *If ye love me, keep my commandments.*

God gave the Ten Commandments as a gift that would keep us on the narrow road. In my life when I walked off this narrow road it always lead to destruction. Well you might say, "now brother we are not under the law or the Ten Commandments". No, that isn't what I am saying. We should live with the Ten Commandments as we live with God. For God did speak these words. But more so if we would live with these Ten Commandments life would be more of a blessing then the hell we live in. Don't you think?

So never love someone more than God our Father, this will help you from getting into a bad relationship or the troubles of life!

By: Evangelist Bill Carter 8/26/04

What causes divorce

God authorized the unity of marriage. ***Therefore if God is not our first love, how can we truly understand love!*** Without God we are only walking in the flesh. Without God we don't have the Holy Spirit. If you don't have the Holy Spirit, you don't have the spirit of God in and around you. We have power in the Holy Spirit! Believe this; you will need the Holy Spirit when the devil comes to destroy your marriage. So without being a Christian how can you Love, or have power to keep your Marriage together? Let's look at what the word flesh means:

FLESH: A word for human contrast to the spirit (Matthew 26:41). The word is also used for unredeemed human nature and carnal appetites or desires which can lead to sin (Galatians 5:16, 17).

The first things that happens before a DIVORCE; there is a break down in unity. Without God in your marriage, you are standing alone inside of your marriage. Without God how can your marriage stand in **UNITY!** The devil seeks out to destroy marriages. It's been said, and I really believe, that the devil will attack the unity of the Family, before he attacks the unity of the church. We can see the effects of divorce in this country. Just about half or more marriages and 54% of Christian marriages today ends in divorce! Without God as our first love, the unity of marriages may be on a path to be **DESTROYED.** Without **GOD,** how can your marriage stand the test of time? The foremost reason for divorces: **MARRIAGE WITHOUT GOD.** (When we leave God out of our life and marriages; we are giving the devil a foothold and control on our lives.) Take out your **BIBLE** and turn to the book of REVELATION. I want to so you a verse about the devil and Satan:

REVELATION 12:9 *And the great dragon was cast out that old serpent, called the devil, and Satan, which deceiveth the whole world: he was cast out into the earth, and his angels were cast out with him.*

Here in this verse in Revelation, we see that the devil and his angels were cast into the earth, to deceive the whole earth or mankind! Now, we are in a real test without God. Not only must we stand against the devil, there are also his fallen angels. Do you think you can take on the devil and his angels without God in your life or marriage? Let's take a look at another verse:

1 PETER 5:8 *Be sober, be vigilant; because your adversary the devil, as a roaring lion, walketh about, seeking whom he may devour:*

The adversary, the devil: along with his fallen angels, are seeking whom he (they) may devour! Does this include you? Yes, it does! That's why we need God in our life and to be a **REAL CHRISTIAN.** Let's look at the words devour, be sober, sober and vigilant:

DEVOUR: to bring to an end by or as if by the action of a destroying force.
BE SOBER: keep a sound mind in God. Self control

SOBER: SENSIBLE, TEMPERATE AND SELF-CONTROLLED: this is an appropriate attitude for believers as we await the Lord's return.

VIGILANT: paying close attention usually with a view to anticipating approaching danger or opportunity.

How much more of a reason do we need, than these last two verses? We need to have and keep God as our first love! We must keep and have God's unity in our marriages, families and churches! When we take God out of the unity structure of marriage; the devil will try to devour your marriage, family or your Christian life?

A notation From Pastor David Atherton: "Union is not Unity". Unless God is a part of the Union! "A marriage without God is a Union of two people, but not a Unity; because God is left out!"

UNITY: continuity without deviation or change (as in purpose or action of Gods plans).

With this understanding of unity, we can see the effects it can have on marriages. Now, think about people you know that have had divorces. Remember there is no unity without God! This means you are standing alone to fight the devil and his fallen angels alone. What happens to marriages without God? What will happen to marriages, and family without the unity of God? Now, we can see the effects of marriages and family without God and without God's unity. No wonder marriages and families are being destroyed. ***We blame everything on the reasons that cause all these divorces. But, we still leave out God, WHY? Now you see what causes divorces, will you marry without God? Now you know the truth about divorces!***

Seven deadly sins

PROVERBS 6:16,17,18,19 *These six things doth the Lord hate: yea, seven are an abomination unto him: A proud look, a lying tongue, and hands that shed innocent blood, A heart that deviseth wicked imaginations, feet that be swift in running to mischief, A false witness that speaketh lies, and he that soweth discord among brethren.*

A lot of people don't have the understanding of this word, abomination. So let's take a look at this word.

ABOMINATION: Something considered repulsive by the Hebrews. Examples of these despised practices are heathen idolatry (Deut. 7:25, 26), blemished animal sacrifices (Deut. 17:1), sexual transgressions (Lev. 18), child sacrifice (Deut. 12:31), and the practices of witchcraft, magic, and spiritism (Deut. 18:9-12). These practices were also regarded as an abomination to God (Lev. 18:26).

Now, let's review these seven deadly sins in Proverbs: The seven things the Lord hates are listed below: The first five being described poetically under the parts of the body associated with a particular sin:
A PROUD LOOK (" PROUD EYES"), A LYING TONGUE, HANDS THAT SHED INNOCENT BLOOD, A HEART THAT DEVISE WICKED IMAGINATION, FEET THAT BE SWIFT IN RUNNING TO MISCHIEF, A FALSE WITNESS, HE THAT SOWETH DISCORD AMONG BRETHREN.

It is clear from the last two items in the list that God is describing people whom he hates. The word hate should not be taken in an absolute sense, however because it means, "to reject from ones fellowship.) These are the kinds of people God rejects. We as Christians should know and keep these seven deadly sins in our heart and mind. So we will never do any of these seven sins! Be not deceived by your flesh or by the devil and his fallen angels! I want to give and show you one other verse in Proverbs:

PROVERBS 9:10 *The fear of the Lord is the beginning of wisdom: And knowledge of the LORD (Holy one) is understanding.* **(The word LORD in this verse means Holy One!)**

GOD'S WISDOM FORMS UNITY

Without the fear of the Lord, there is no wisdom! Where there is no wisdom, how can there be any unity? We need this Holy understanding about the fear of the Lord. If you or yours can't live by God's words there will never be any unity in a marriage, family or your Christian life! Therefore what good is marriage without God? Would you marry if you knew it would fail? Let me ask you one more time, **WOULD YOU MARRY IF YOU KNEW IT WOULD FAIL?**
So that you don't have an unhappy marriage put **JESUS IN YOUR LIFE AND MARRIAGE!**

By: *Evangelist Bill Carter 9/99*

We must know when the thief cometh

John 10:10 *The thief (Satan) cometh not, but for to steal, and to kill, and to destroy: I am come (Jesus) that they might have life, and that they might have it more abundantly.*

1: Who is the **thief** in this verse? *Satan is the thief!*
2: What does the thief **steal**? *Your finances and material blessing!*
3: What does the thief **kill**? *The family!*
4: Who does the thief try to **destroy**? *You and everyone else that is a Christian!*
5: What did **Jesus** come to do for the Christian? *Jesus has come that we would have life and that we might have it more abundantly! Praise God!*

John 10:11 *I am the good shepherd: the good shepherd giveth His life for the sheep.*

In this verse, Jesus gives His life for every follower and believer in Him. **Jesus** calls Himself the **GOOD SHEPHERD!** This is why we must take a stand with Jesus, when Satan comes to steal, kill and to destroy. We must tell him, "get away from us Satan, Jesus is our Shepherd."

Now I want you to recall Job. What did Satan do to Job? If you have never studied the book of Job, you need to! Satan took Job's wealth and finances, Satan came to steal from Job. What did Satan kill concerning Job? His family! Now whom did Satan try to destroy? Job! This paragraph shows what Satan did to Job. You as a Christian should know what the thief is up to. This is why we should read and study the book of Job from time to time. Then when the thief comes we can count our blessings in the Good Shepherd.

This is the most overlooked verse in the book of Job:
Job 42:1-2 *Then Job answered the Lord, and said, Vs. 2: I know that thou canst do every thing, and that no thought can be withholden from thee.*

Who can do everything? The Lord can, amen! We cannot hide our thoughts from the Lord! I want to show you a list of things we should know and be doing as Christian.

1 Thessalonians 5:16-24 *Rejoice evermore. Vs. 17 Pray without ceasing. Vs. 18 In every thing give thanks: for this is the will of God in Christ Jesus concerning you. Vs. 19 Quench not the spirit. Vs. 20 Despise not prophesyings. Vs. 21 Prove all things; hold fast that which is good. Vs. 22 Abstain from all appearance of evil. Vs. 23 And the very God of peace sanctify you wholly; and I Pray God your whole spirit and soul and body be preserved blameless unto the coming of our Lord Jesus Christ. Vs. 24 <u>Faithful is he that calleth you, who also will do it.</u>* The Holy Spirit gave this to me the night I went to the hospital to receive four pints of blood.
I prayed I would go home in three days in good health, and I did!
Jesus is the Good Shepherd

By: Evangelist Bill Carter 4/8/03 **

Peace

There are times when we all seek peace. I get like this as well. But God gave us peace and to attain it may be hard if we don't look for peace from God. I know at times our peace is taken from us. But, the Lord restores our peace.

John 14:27 *Peace I leave with you, my peace I give unto you: not as the world giveth, give I unto you. Let not your heart be troubled, neither let it be afraid.*

Peace is what Jesus left with us. In John 14:28, Jesus talks about the comforter, which is the Holy Ghost. Jesus goes on to say in verse 27, my peace I give unto you. This is why we shouldn't let our hearts, be troubled, neither let it be afraid. Turn to the book of Romans.

Romans 5:1-2 *Therefore being justified by faith, we have peace with God through our Lord Jesus Christ. By whom also we have access by faith into this grace wherein we stand, and rejoice in hope of the glory of God.*

We are justified by faith. **Yes, the test of life is tough at times. But we must keep the faith.** If we don't, we may lose all peace that God has given us through our Lord Jesus Christ. **This faith gives us, access to the grace given to us by Jesus. No matter where we stand. That is why we must rejoice in the hope of the glory of God.**

Romans 15:13 *Now the God of hope fill you with all joy and peace in believing, that ye may abound in hope, through the power of the Holy Ghost.*

Here is where we see the power of the Holy Ghost. Look what God does for us. **God fills us with, all joy and peace in believing that we may abound in hope.** How can this be, through the power of the Holy Ghost!

Romans 8:28 And we know that all things work together for good to them that love God, to them who are the called according to his purpose.

The first part of verse 28 said it all. We know that all things work together for good to them that love God.

Isaiah 26:3-4 *Thou wilt keep him in perfect peace, whose mind is stayed on thee: because he trusteth in thee. vs.4: Trust ye in the Lord for ever: for in the Lord Jehovah is everlasting strength.*

If we keep our mind on the Lord, God will keep us in perfect peace. How long should we trust in the Lord? Forever, that's how long. **Look at how long the Lords' strength is for us. It is an everlasting strength!!**

John 16:33 *These things I have spoken unto you, that in me ye might have peace. In the world ye shall have tribulation: But be of good cheer; I have overcome the world.*

Jesus is speaking here. Jesus has spoken about the peace we have in Him. But, Jesus also tells us; in this world we shall have tribulation. **But, here is the peace of our tribulation. But be of good cheer; I (Jesus) have overcome the world. This is the blessing and peace we have in Jesus, Amen!**

By: Evangelist Bill Carter3/15/01

When we are being Defensive

Defensive: 1: Serving to defend or protect. 2: Devoted to resisting or preventing aggression or attack. **(Defensive - 2):** a defensive position - on the defensive: in the state or condition of being prepared for an expected aggression or attack.

Being defensive is not being a good Christian, unless you're at war. That war can be spiritual! If you're in a spiritual war and you become defensive to your family, loved one, friends, Christians, the Godhead, or the church. *Whose side are you on? Is this of God or Satan?* You need to know it's one of the two, who is it? ***If God be for you, who can be against you?*** So why would you become defensive at your family, loved ones, Christians, the Godhead or the church? If you're a Christian act like it!
Therefore if you are being defensive against your family, love ones, friends, Christians, the God- head or the church. ***You're being doubled minded!*** Christians are not to be doubled minded!

James 1: 1 - 9: *Vs. 1: James a servant of God and of the Lord Jesus Christ, to the twelve tribes which are scattered abroad, greetings. Vs. 2: My brethren, count it all joy when ye fall into divers temptations; Vs. 3: Knowing this, that the trying (testing) of your faith worketh patience. Vs. 4: But let patience have her perfect work, that ye may be perfect (complete) and entire, wanting (lacking) nothing. Vs. 5: If any of you lack wisdom, let him ask of God, that giveth to all men liberally, and upbraideth not; and it shall be given him. Vs. 6: But let him ask in faith, nothing wavering (not doubting). For he that wavereth (doubts) is like a wave of sea driven with the wind and tossed. Vs. 7: For let not that man think that he shall receive any thing of the Lord. Vs. 8:* **A double-minded man (or women) is unstable in all his (her) ways.** *Vs. 9: Let the brother (sister) of low degree rejoice in that he (she) is exalted.*

To all of you that are being treated by someone who is being defensive, rejoice in him or her and exalt them in prayer and in heart. **Love conquers all sin!** *Love is forgiveness and understanding, this always applies to love!* (Remember that we all can do things and say things that we didn't really mean)! ***Watch this: (I ask you to forgive me)! Why? If we have faith then by faith we should forgive one another for this is the will of God, Amen! So, when you're being defensive you're really hurting the Kingdom of God! Don't ever forget this!***

When you are being defensive you are oppressed and you are in a spiritual war. I ask you again whose side are you on. If you're oppressed with something, go to war spiritually with that! Not your brothers or sisters! ***Oppression is not of God!***

Timothy1:6-8 *Vs.6: Wherefore I put thee in remembrance that thou stir up the gift of God, which is in thee by the putting on of my hands.*
Vs.7: **For God hath not given us the spirit of fear; but of power, and love, and a sound mind.** *Vs. 8: Be not thou therefore ashamed of the testimony of our Lord, nor of me his*

prisoner: but be thou partaker of the afflictions of the gospel according to the power of God. Vs. 9: Who hath saved us, and called us with a holy calling, not according to our works, but according to his own purpose and grace, which was given us in Christ Jesus before the world began,

John 14:26-27 *But the <u>comforter (helper), which is the Holy Ghost,</u> whom the Father will send in my name (Jesus), He shall teach you all things, and bring all things to your remembrance, whatsoever I have said unto you. Vs. 27:* **Peace I leave with you, my peace I give unto you: not as the world giveth, give I unto you. Let not your heart be troubled, neither let it be afraid.**

Romans 8:14-16 *Vs. 14: For as many as are led by the Spirit of God, they are the sons (and daughters) of God. Vs.* **15: For ye have not received the spirit of bondage again to fear; but ye have received the Spirit of adoption, whereby we cry, <u>Abba Father</u> Vs. 16 The Spirit itself beareth witness with our spirit, <u>that we are the child of God.</u>**

In viewing these verses that you just read, I hope that you find freedom from your oppression of being defensive.

When we say things that are not need, we are just making worthless talk or vain babbling. That is why we should study to show ourself, to be in the will of our Father God! Look at this verse in:

2 Timothy 2: 14-17 *Of these things put them in remembrance, charging them before the Lord that they strive not about words to no profit, but to the subverting (ruin) of hearers. Vs. 15:Study to show thyself approved unto God, a workman that needeth not to be ashamed, rightly dividing the word of truth. Vs. 16:* **<u>But shun profane and vain babblings: for this will increase unto more ungodliness</u>**. *Vs. 17;* **<u>And their word will eat (spread) as doth a canker (cancer</u>**): *of whom is Hymeneus and Philetus;*

Hymeneus is the one whom Paul delivered to Satan. Hymeneus and Philetus were false teachers who denied the literal resurrection of Christ. **If you're being defensive against your family and love ones, you are a discord in the eyes of our Father God**. If you get anything out of this next verse, get this, for a remembrance!
> **When you're being defensive are you being a discord among your brotherhood?**
> **Now when you're being defensive whose side are you on? God our Father or Satan,**
> **It's your choice!**

By: Evangelist Bill Carter 1/6/04

Trying to get back to a past relationship

You're not going to find this in a Single Christian book. This may be the hardest subject to write on. Some might think this shouldn't be brought up all. How do we try to get back to the person that may have been God sent? What would you do if someone told you they believe that God may have put us together and you messed the relationship up? This is about truth not judgment! If a person is trying to get back with you, take time to listen to them and what God may be doing. But if you know this past relationship was not God sent just move on! *Single adults need to marry, not make more mistakes! Now that I have your full attention, this is where the truth must come into play. This is about courage and respect. Faith can't be seen!*

Hebrews 11:1 *Now faith is the substance of things hoped for, the evidence of things not seen.*

This may be the chance you have been praying for. Does God our Father give us a 2nd chance? **Yes, but there is one thing that God our Father will not do. That is, God will not change the free will of someone. You shouldn't try to change the free will of someone!** But yes, it's ok to try to get back with someone even if you messed things up; but this must be done will all due respect! You should not do this without praying. Stop here if you are trying to get back with someone and pray this prayer.

Father God, this hour I come to you asking and seeking the truth about this past relationship (Call that person by name: _____). Father, I'm not trying to change the will of this person. I'm only trying to see if you have put us together. Allow me to do this with all due respect for this person and you Father God! Let your will be done. I ask this in the name of Jesus, AMEN!

DID YOU WALK AWAY FROM
WHAT GOD HAD SENT YOU?

This is where you need to open your heart to this writing. **You must come to terms with three things, respect, trust and faith.** A past relationship may not work out. There is a chance for rejection, as you try to get this past relationship started again. If you were the one left behind you still have a right to try. Whether you left or were left behind and you want to try to restore a past relationship. *You will have to be justifiable on this issue.* If you left someone and you hurt them, believe me this will be next to impossible! What if you were the one left behind, it's just as hard. Remember this; the truth will set you free. DON'T TAKE REJECTION AS A FAILER. IT MAY BE BEST FOR YOU. THIS MAYBE HARD TO TAKE IN AND THIS IS WHERE FAITH COMES IN. Ok, are you ready for action? Faith without action is dead!

You walked away from your soul mate. Or the soul mate walked away from you. I'm going to repeat myself here. ***Single adults need to marry, not make mistakes! If you're the one who is approached take time in listening to that person. Don't say anything at first. This is a time that the two of you need to seek GOD our Father. If the two of you had sex you need to wait on God about this issue. If you two are to be together the truth will come out. Pride will kill what God was trying to do.*** Did you walk away from what God had sent you to find greener grass? **I WOULD TRADE ALL THE GREEN GRASS OF THIS WORLD TO LAY IN A SOFT PLACE CALLED MARRIAGE!** <u>***Would you?***</u> *If you are approached please take the time to think about this, give it thirty days or so, as you pray. Unless you know this was not God sent!* Ask that person to wait on the Lord just like you are doing. Don't get your hope up here, but keep your Faith in God. *Your faith may lead you to move on. This is where having faith turns into a blessing.*

This is where it's going to get hard. There may be some pain in doing this. ***You need to be ready for this. There will be a lot of questions to answer here.*** Let's see if you are ready to put a relationship back to gather!
 Steps to take:
- This must be done by faith not by flesh
- This is a step of respect not judgment
- We can't change the will of someone
- This is a time to pray and seek God our Father
- Put it in God's hands, not yours
- Study the Bible
- This will take some time to see what will happen
- This is where the truth needs to be the truth
- Don't keep asking or chasing at all

<u>**Proverbs 3:5-6**</u> *Trust in the LORD with all thine heart; and lean not unto thine own understanding. In all thy ways acknowledge him, and he shall direct thy paths.*

<u>**Psalm 20:7**</u> *Offer the sacrifices of righteousness, and put your trust in the LORD.*

<u>**Proverbs 30:5**</u> *Every word of God is Pure: he (GOD) is a shield unto them that put their trust in him.*

<u>***If you want to try to put a past relationship back together, do you have the faith?***</u>
Rejection stands at the door. From your heart take a deep look at these next few things I'm going to outline for you.
- Ask God to forgive you and the other person
- Are you sure this person was your soul mate
- Why did you leave this person or why did they leave you
- How did you hurt this person or how were you hurt

- Are you willing to listen and tell the truth about your relationship
- Can you prove to yourself that you can be true
- Can you become friends again
- The other person may be in another relationship
- Can you talk about your mistakes and sins
- This may be the hardest thing you can do, can you outline the relationship you want with this person
- Are you willing to accept rejection of trying
- Can you use this as a chance to ask for forgiveness
- You must be able to answer all question with the truth and from your heart

These are just a few things to think about.

Now that you're sure you walked away from your soul mate and you still want to try to get back together. Do you want to restore that past relationship? Once again I have outlined a few things to do in full respect of the other person. *Remember keep the faith, keep the respect and don't try to change the will of someone at all!*

1: Send a nice card with your name on it, ask them to call; if they don't call you have the answer.
2: Small gift like: flowers, balloon, candy or tickets.
3: Here is where we need to be able to except rejection. If they don't call or want to talk, it's over.
4: I want you to have a clear understanding here: You should never ever call that person at work. Contact them by mail is the best way, (home or cell) phone only or e-mail.

1Peter 2:17 *Honor all men (women). Love the brotherhood. Fear God Honor the king (Jesus Christ).*

Matthew 5:4 *Blessed are they that mourn: For they shall be comforted.*

By: Evangelist Bill Carter
8/17/04

Study the Bible

This is one of the **New Testaments** commandments. So, if you would open your Bible to, 2 Timothy Chapter 2.

2 timothy 2:15 *Study to show thyself approve unto God, a workman that needeth not to be ashamed, rightly dividing the word of truth.*

As we take a look at verse 15, ask yourself, why should we study the Bible?
Study: means "give diligence, be diligent, and zealous". It involves a total effort of mind, emotion, and will.
Show: present, show, exhibit, display, expose, parade, flaunt, and means to present so as to invite notice or attention. Show implies no more that enabling another to see or examine, evidence suggests serving as proof of the actuality or existence of something, (manifest, demonstrate).
Rightly Dividing: (cutting straight) the word of truth, Paul the apostle of Jesus Christ. Is saying here, we need to make a great effort to properly interpret the Word of God.

Ok, now you know that this is a commandment. We must take great efforts in studying the Bible. When I read some of the Christian studies, they suggest, that only 10 to 20 percent of Christians read their Bible. And only 5 to 10 percent study the Bible. DO YOU READ OR STUDY THE BIBLE?

2 timothy 2:16 but *shun profane and vain babblings: for they will increase unto more ungodliness.*

Let's look at some of these words in verse 16.
Vain babblings: worthless talk refers to useless disputes (over anything) like genealogical, histories and debates over the law. This type of conversation, are just saying things that are totaly useless!
Vain: empty, empty sounding, and fruitless discussion.
Profane: heathenish (deliberatively insults), wicked, profane person.

We are responsible for what comes out of our mouth. You can laugh at this all you want to but, I ask you are you a person that does vain babblings? If you had studied your Bible you would have known to keep your mouth in control! *Study the Bible; it holds the truth and the Words of God.* There is nothing of value in profane and vain babblings; they lead to UNGODLINESS!

By: Evangelist Bill Carter 9/2/00

Finding things to do on a budget

This is important in building a relationship. Couples must have a budget!
It's a real mistake to live outside your budget!
Yes there are a lot of things you can do working with a budget!
These activities still can be fun and romantic!

I have written out a few things you and yours can do on a budget. You don't have to spend a lot of money to have quality actives. **Your enjoyment should come out of your love for each other. Not your expectation!**

**But remember it is your actives,
that will help keep your relationship
live and well.**
Simple Ideas

Playing cards, Darts, Game boards have been around for a long time, Art, Playing music, Cookouts, Cooking, Health Food cooking, Special movies, Take each other out on a date, Supporting each other hobbies, Walking, Biking, Fitness program, Church actives, is always a great thing for couples to get into,

Join a Church cell group, or bible study, Prayer time, Pick a night that you can be romantic, Learn about outdoor actives like: Canoeing, fishing, hunting, skiing, exploring cave, rappelling, skydiving; this list could be much longer and I ask you to think of some activities. Always think of your mate!

This is such a small list but this will make you think.
It's ok to have a budget. It's not ok, not to have a budget!

It's so important to plan your activities. You owe it to your relationship and marriage. Support each other's hobbies or just something your companion likes to do. Yes, you even may have to learn to like something. But it's not as bad as you allow it to be. You will always have a need to support your partner.

This is where a lot of couples miss the mark in activities for their relationship. When you don't spend time in this area of your relationship, you may find your relationship fading. It takes a lot to keep a relationship alive. But it only takes a few things to allow a relationship to fade away and die.

Great activities will create a health relationship.

Why I love you

This is only my point of view and views from some of my friends. So here's a chance to see what a quality single man and women looks for. *We all know how hard it is to find love, but it's even harder to find a companionship love.* This list is short and just a point of view that has no order.

Your smile, you are smart, I don't have to baby sit you, I trust you and you trust me, I'm attracted to you, you're a lot of fun, you care about me, you say what you mean and mean what you say, no head games, I like the activities we do together, we like to travel, watching movies together alone, the will to accept changes, manhood with you, womanhood with you, you can forgive, your understanding, you have great conversation, you are not boring, really romantic, great companions, you understand companionship, you believe in me, you would be a great help mate, you have a heart that can love, I love the way you look at me, you talk about your future (goals, desires and wants), you listen, your flexibility, you have wisdom, you let me grow in love, you grew in love, and we were friends first then we became companions. But more so you are a man or woman that prays!

Write out some things that make you feel you love a person.

_____

_____

_____

_____

_____

_____

_____

_____

_____

_____

_____

_____

_____

_____

_____

_____

Beware of one's body language

Body language: the gestures and mannerisms by which a person communicates with one's body. Body language can show signs of behavior problems or issues. Body language can also show signs of quality behaviors or issues.

Communication skills and Body language = People skills

I just want to make you aware of body language. It is part of the makeup as a person. Body language will allow you to see a person for who they really are. ***When body language goes along with their communication skills at the beginning, you are looking at a person who is being them self. And if their body language is different than their communication skill, there is a reason for this.*** Remember, you must take time to know someone. *People will use their body language first before they use their Communication skills.* ***When a quality person has good body gestures, it shows. When a person has aggression in their body language, this will give you the first sign of trouble.*** Body language will happen before poor communications skills. Everyone can speak nice. But most people don't control their body language.

Signs to look for when someone has aggression: Hitting things, pointing fingers, hold up their hands a lot, faking hitting things including people, kicking things, fake kicking, grabbing, biting their lip, tongue, fingers and so on. These are just a few signs. ***Most people that have body language aggression have real habits, with their gestures. Habits can be a warning.***
Signs to look for when someone has quality behaviors: hugs, hand shake, look at you when they talk with happiness, waves, smile, signs of peace, look like they are listening; these are just a few things.

There is a lot to say about this subject. You really have to come to know someone, in order to understand one's body language. That's another reason to take your time in a relationship. ***It may take 30 to 60 days for a person to act normal. But in time you will see their body language.***

Note your body language:

_____

_____

_____

_____

_____

_____

_____

Your Salvation / read the book of Romans

I can't end this book without asking about your salvation. Paul stated that we should work out our own salvation. (*Philippians 2:12 Wherefore, my beloved, as ye have always obeyed, not as in my presence only, but now much more in my absence, work out your own salvation with fear and trembling.*) I want you to read the book of Romans. Who is Paul talking to in Romans chapter one? You can find this information out in Romans 1:7 (he is talking to the saints) or (beloved of God), the Christians at Rome. Open your Bible to Romans chapter one. This is a small chapter, read this chapter for yourselves; there are many Bible verses, which teach us about back siding, sin and to repent. If you are not aware of these Bible verses; you should study the bible. Find these verses and keep them in your heart. **So where are you with your salvation?**

If you where standing in front of Jesus.
And Jesus started to talk with you.
How would you act?
Then Jesus Himself asked you.
If you would accept
The gift of grace,
That brings forth salvation!
What would your answer be?
Yes or No?
The Bible makes it clear.
You have already been asked!
So what is your answer?
Then Jesus asked you one other question.
Would it be better to be a Christian or not to be a Christian?
How would you answer this question?
You know the truth.
The truth will inform you and change you.
The truth will set you free,
Salvation is through our
Lord and King
Jesus Christ.

If you are not saved, go to a church and talk with a Pastor.
You need a church and a Pastor.
This will help build a greater foundation as a Christian.
Church is a great place to meet single adults!
I could type out all the Bible verse about salvation.
But it's between God and you.
You're the one that needs to study the Bible.

The Bible will give you the peace you need!

WATER BAPTISM

When we accept salvation, through our Lord Jesus Christ; it is very important to take steps that will help to identify us with Christ, in <u>every area</u> of our life as a Christian. After we have accepted the gift of salvation, our next step as New Christians should be Water Baptism. This is a powerful way, which New Believers can be identified with Christ.

<u>Matthew 28:18-20</u> *And Jesus came and spake unto them, saying,* **All power is given unto me in heaven and in earth.** *vs. 19:* **Go ye therefore, and teach all nations, baptizing them in the name of the Father, and of the Son, and of the Holy Ghost:** *vs. 20:* **Teaching them to observe all things whatsoever I have commanded you: and, lo, I am with you always, even unto the end of the world, Amen.**

Now let's look at these three verses: Who is speaking here? Jesus is speaking here! The statement in verse 18, (all power is given to me) the word **Power** in this verse means **Authority**. All authority is given to Jesus Christ, in heaven and in earth. Now look at verse 19, Go ye therefore and teach all nations, **which is imply to everyone.** What are we to teach them? To be baptized in the name of the Father, and the Son, and the Holy Ghost. Then in Verse 20: Jesus Christ was telling them to **Observe all things whatsoever I have commanded you**. Now is Water Baptism a commandment? I think so! When Jesus said, I am with you always. He states what he means, **even unto the end of the world, Amen.**

Let's look at one other verse in the book of Acts: **(read chapter 8)**
<u>Acts 8:12</u> *But when they believed Philip preaching, the things concerning the kingdom of God, and the name of Jesus Christ, they were baptized, both men and women.*

Who was baptized? The **believers**, both **men** and **women!**

Turn your Bible to the book of Mark. Jesus is talking about Baptism in this last chapter of this book as well.

Mark 16: 15 -16 *And he said unto them,* **Go ye into all the world, and preach the gospel to every creature.** *vs. 16:* **He that believeth and is baptized shall be saved; but he that believeth not shall be damned.**

Look at how verse 16 starts out, but look at how it ends. What happens to them that believeth not? They shall be **DAMNED!** *That is why we should take a deep look at this. I ask you once more, is this a commandment?*

By now you might be thinking this is getting deep. Let me show you how deep Jesus Christ was immersed at His baptism.

Matthew 3:16-17 *And Jesus, when he was baptized,* **went up straightway out of the water:** *and, lo, the heavens were opened unto him, and he saw the Spirit of God descending like a dove, and lighting upon him: vs. 17: And lo a voice from heaven, saying,* **This is my beloved Son, in whom I am well pleased.**

Mark 1:9-11 *And it came to pass in those days, that Jesus came from Nazareth of Galilee, and was Baptized of John in Jordan. vs. 10:* **And straightway coming up out of the water**, *he saw the heavens opened, and the Spirit like a dove descending upon him. vs. 11: And there came a voice from heaven, saying,* **Thou art my beloved Son, in whom I am well pleased.**

I want to show you two things in these two books of Matthew and Mark:
1: Matthew: WENT UP STRAIGHTWAY OUT OF THE WATER!
Mark: AND STRAIGHTWAY COMING UP OUT OF THE WATER!

How did Jesus come out of the water? **Straightway!** Does this mean he stood up out of the water? **Yes!** If Jesus came up out of the water does this mean he was immersed? Well let's look up the word to see what it means:

{Webster's Ninth New Collegiate Dictionary}
Baptize: *to dip, dipped, to purify or cleanse spiritually*

{Nelson's, the New Strong's Exhaustive Concordance of Bible}
Baptized: (Greek) 907 baptizo: from a der. 911; to make overwhelmed (i.e. *fully wet*) used only (in the N.T.) the ordinance of Christian *baptism:* baptist. baptize, **wash.**
911 bapto: a primary verb; to *overwhelm*, i.e. **cover wholly with a fluid**; in the N.T. only in a qualified or special sense, i.e. (lit.) to *moisten* (a part of one's person), or (by impl.) to *stain* (as with dye):-**dip.**

Baptism means: *the process of immersion or to be fully wet, dip, dipped!*

Now what did God Himself say about Jesus when he was Baptized? This is my beloved Son, in whom I am well pleased. Thou art my beloved Son, in whom I am well pleased.
Now if God Himself was well pleased in Jesus for doing this. And if we are to be Christ like,

shouldn't we be immersed under the water as well? *Yes, In the name of Father, and of the Son, and of the Holy Ghost!*

In baptism, the immersion of the believer symbolized his death to sin and his resurrection to the new life he or she now has in Christ, Amen! **Objects are submerged; People are immersed!**

Romans 6: 3-6 *Know ye not, that so many of us as were baptized into Jesus Christ were baptized into his death? vs. 4: Therefore we are buried with him by baptism into death: that like as Christ was raised up from the dead by the glory of the Father, even so we also should walk in newness of life. vs:5: For if we have been planted together in the likeness of his death, we shall be also in the likeness of his resurrection: vs. 6: Knowing this, that our old man is crucified with him, that the body of sin might be destroyed, that henceforth we should not, serve sin.*

To save a little time I'm not going to break down these verses. But ask that you read and study them. I only want to bring out one point, that we as Christians over look. In verse six: ***that henceforth we should not, serve sin. The word serve here means (be slaves of -sin)!***

1 Peter 3:21 *The like figure whereunto even baptism doth also now save us (not the putting away of the filth of the flesh, but the answer of a good conscience toward God,) by the resurrection of Jesus Christ:*

A NEW MAN OR NEW WOMEN

As you come up out of the water, your baptism confirms the fact that your old sinful nature has been crucified and that you have put on a new godly nature. You have made a new commitment to serve Jesus Christ. You have separated yourself from the old sinful nature and life style.

By: Evangelist Bill Carter **2/26/03

Notes:

_____
_____
_____
_____
_____
_____
_____
_____
_____

Trial of Faith

Faith isn't so hard if we keep it alive. If we keep God's love in our heart, faith will only grow. Faith is much like love, if you don't let it grow, it will die! Does faith grow, yes? The more you learn about the Godhead, your faith will grow with time and knowledge. Love grows from time and knowledge of someone. The longer you spend with someone, the more knowledge you have of them, yourself and the relationship.

In the subjects you read in this book, how has it affected you? I hope it has made you think about yourself and relationship behaviors. Now, more than ever, you need to build up your faith in God, Jesus, and the Holy Spirit.

You now your mistakes and the changes you need to make in your life. You future is ahead of you. There is someone out there for you. Don't fall in love, allow love to grow in your next relationship. Take your time in doing so.
People say that matches are made in heaven. Are they? A lady was asking, "do you think God will send me a Christian?" That is all he has! *Look for a Christian that is willing to learn about a Christian life. This will help you in your relationship.* Remember you are not perfect, neither is the one you find for a companion. *Don't try to change a person, leave this up to your prayers, love and God. That's a real step of faith. Change takes time, doesn't it? If you have to make a point, be clear and humble!*

Let all changes be a reflection of your relationship growth.

1Peter 1:7
That the trial of your faith, being much more precious than of gold that perisheth, though it be tried with fire...

Mark 11:22
And Jesus answering saith unto them, Have faith in God.

Amos 3:3
Can two walk together, except they be agreed?

Think about it

I hope this book and its many subjects, has given you the opportunity to think about relationships and companionships. It's with my greatest attention to awaken you to change for yourself. You have the rest of your life ahead of you. Today you must decide the path you will take. All roads lead to somewhere. But the question is where are you taking yourself? There is no short cut to any relationship growth.

If you are broken hearted take your time in your recovery. You owe this to yourself and family members.
From time to time pickup this book and read the subjects you need. Look at the Bible verses and keep them in your heart. Make notes to yourself and others. Remember if you are blessing, you are a blessing.

Give this book to a friend in need of help

How many times have you heard yourself or others say,
I wish I could help so and so?
Well give them this book!
There are a lot of Bible verses,
That could give them the peace they are looking for.
You may not have the time or knowledge to help someone.
I feel this book could bless a lot of single adults.
As I took the time to write out so many subjects,
Each one of these subjects was prayed over.
Allow this book to give you
Peace after your Broken Relationship

Living together versus marriage

Living together: This is only a temporary ideal; it does not bring forth the companionship of a family unit! I chose to use the word temporary to those who chose to live together. I did this for a few reasons.

1: Living together has no real foundation of commitment. This type of commitment is day by day and may last a few years at the most. Not a lifetime.

2: There is no oneness in living together; the two people will live under established rules. There is no unity in their companionship, just titles and union.

3: More than likely one of the two will be used as a "hang around person."

4: There is no home; it's just a house.

5: What is yours is yours and what is theirs is theirs. Everything is singled out, without any unity.

6: For the most love doesn't grow into marriage or companionship. One may be happy where this type of relationship. If love doesn't keep growing it just dies! This is what happen to living together.

7: Living together is just temporary, and day by day. There is no commitment for a lifetime of companionship!

8: The relationship love may never grow into companionship love.

9: When God gave the gift of marriage, he took two people and made them one in unity. This cannot happen when you choose to live together; it just a union!

10: There is a real difference in companionship love in marriage, versus the love that's in a live together life style!

Here are a few statements, made by people who live together.

- <u>Why buy the milk when it's free</u>. *What I have said to that statement is; Love that is real will grow toward marriage. For marriage was given as a free gift from God Himself!*
- <u>We are living together to see if it will work.</u> *So where is the real commitment? I say; work toward marriage and allow your love and commitment to grow and stay alive! That is worth working for. You are blessed when you enter marriage.*
- <u>I have fear in marriage</u>. *What you are really saying is this; "I'm not committed to marriage," or "I don't have the knowledge of a real companionship relation."*
- <u>We haven't made a pre marriage agreement.</u> *I say to you get an attorney that can help you!*

- <u>You say it will not work.</u> *I say, it takes a lot of work, and you have no commitment!*
- <u>It's cheaper to live together than live single.</u> *This is a true statement, that's why God said two is better than one. Marriage is God's plan! A man needs a woman, as much as a woman needs a man. Companionship in marriage can and will save the two of you a lot of money and time.*
- <u>I just want someone to be here or a hang person.</u> *This is one of the greatest mistakes we see with live in couples. You may be living with someone until they get over their issues like; debit, loneliness, depression, sexual lifestyle, change in life, help fix up my house and so on. My question to you; are being used?*
- If someone does believe in marriage there may be few reasons for this. Like: they really don't love you; just have you in their life until they think they have met someone else that they think is better; doesn't understand love or can't love; they don't want to answer to a relationship lifestyle and so on.

List some of your reason why you don't believe in Marriage.

_____
_____
_____
_____
_____
_____
_____
_____
_____
_____
_____
_____
_____
_____
_____
_____
_____
_____
_____
_____

Which is better? Marriage or living together! The answer is in your heart!

From the past to the future

When we live in the past we have no future!

There are so many people who cannot truly forget their past. They can't forgive their past mistakes or other people that have befriended them. *In life we must walk after the truth, not our expectations or imaginations.* We must be able to forgive ourselves and other people. Without forgiveness we may not have a future. The walls that we build are the same walls we will have to take down. The longer your walls stand in front of your future, the harder and colder they become. The harder they become the harder they are to take down. The colder they become the less likely you are to take them down.

So I ask you to warm your hearts with the hope and faith of your future; with love that comes only through forgiveness. This starts with you; we must forgive ourselves, before we can forgive other people. Love can and will forgive all sins. But we must love ourselves first!

From the past to the future, this is your walk of life. *If you walk toward the future you must learn and have the knowledge of relationship growth.* Without this you may end up walking in circles. *When we walk in circles we always come back to the same places. When we walk in a narrow path, we walk in truth and toward our future.* So where are you walking, in circles or the narrow path? **The paths that one walks will determine where one will end up in life.** I ask you to choose this day to walk after the truth and the narrow path. Knowledge is this same path that I speak of. *Please read (Mathew 7:13, 14 that talks about the narrow and wide path.)*

Knowledge will allow you to seek experiences.
This will allow you to grow toward your future.
You must allow your mistakes to become tools of success!
Success only comes from trying.
Failure comes from trying as well.
But keep trying!
We must learn from this statement,
I have made a lot of mistakes, but, I have not failed!
This is what it takes to become successful!

Working toward a committed relationship

This is what all single adults should do. Work toward a committed relationship! In all that I wrote in this book I'm asking all that reads this book; to work toward a real committed relationship. I showed you a lot of things about yourself and your past relationship.
It is up to you to pray and take action in having a great relationship.

So I ask you to take the needed steps to get on with your life and find the companion you have prayed for. I hope you support your local church and single ministries. I can only ask you, to live as a Christian. **You have tried everything else; why not try to live as a Christian.** Is this hard to do? Yes, but it is your choice. Heaven and hell are real places. On the Day of Judgment, we will all have to face where we spend eternity!

It's with my prayers and hope that you will take in this teaching and be blessed. I ask you to pass this book on to your friends and love ones.

Leap of Faith

Love is hard to find

Each of us has choices

A reason is given to believe

Putting faith toward real love

Opportunity of a lifetime

Friends can become companions

For we have a lot of tomorrows

Another reason to believe

I'm willing to give you my heart

The truth is can you

Having faith, in a real commitment

By: Bill Carter
9|2|07

Relationship

Real opportunity to see if you and I are a match.

Easier said than done!

Letting each other be themselves!

A friend, not a title!

To see if love will grow!

In all that we do and become, let's put God first!

Oh, we should try to see if our goals match!

New relationships are fun. So are you the one?

Seeing is believing; so what direction are we going in?

Have you thought this over, before you make a commitment?

It should be a pleasure, not a mishap!

Putting trust before love!

There are a lot of things one can say about a new relationship. These twelve letters form a great word that most people are looking for! While searching for this, they neglect the structure of this word! *Our imagination may give us an artificial relationship.* We must establish the truth.

We must be able to face the truth in our relationship. Why, we can't change the truth! We must learn to live with a real commitment to God and our companionship. If love doesn't grow it will die. If we grow in love, this will allow love to keep growing (this is faith.) This is where we find real relationships. Remember this always; don't love anyone more than God. This is where you will find the truth and the cornerstones in your relationship.

There are four cornerstones to companionship and marriage.
*Truth * Faith * Companionship * God's unity in marriage*
Companions must always pray
for this is the foundation for the
Cornerstones!

By: Bill Carter
12/23/06
COB Speicher, Tikrit Iraq

Part Four

Open Group Leadership
This part of the book is for group Leadership
Designed to develop you as a leader for this teaching.

If you are leading a group allow yourself time to study this part of the book and other leadership books; (John Maxwell has great books).

If you are working in a ministry of a church make sure you follow the guidelines of your Pastor. If you are working in a jail or prison ministry make sure you have a Pastor and work with the Chaplain of that jail or prison ministry (there maybe rules to follow). We as Christians should sit under the leadership of a Pastor even if we are doing community, public teaching or home groups! If you are a person in the ministry you should still have a Pastor; we all need to be accountable to someone if not a few good Godly Pastors or Elders. You should have someone working with you that will be a witness. I believe single adults should work with the same sex; man should work with man and women work with women. If you are married keep your spouse at your side, as a witness.
I said this to protect you.

There are a few things you will have to be very aware of.
Sexual predators, people that mean to harm someone from a past relationship, Emotions of hurt, Confessions (don't disclose anyone's confession) - they may be trying to heal. Guilt, Depression, Someone trying to take over the meetings, People may become attached to you, drugs and alcohol abuse, the spirit of confusion, You may find yourself without the answers; this is why you need a Pastor! Never fake anything! ***It's up to you to recognize trouble before it starts.***

You can have a greater understanding of Leadership and Ministry training.
If, your Pastor has asked you to get training / education, or has asked you go to another single adult program for a while; do so! You should write out your ministry program, set goals and allow the Pastor to understand what your ministry program and goals are about! ***If you think that's a lot of work you don't need to be a leader of a ministry program!*** If the pastor disagrees with your program or goals, ask for his advice and if the Pastor chooses not to have this type of program; accept this as a blessing! The Pastor is ultimately responsible for all that is taught in the church.

I want everyone to know, how time consuming it is to run a ministry program. Ministry programs are not easy and must be well planned. They also come with a great cost. *You will have to form a great team!*

85

Team Building
Notes from my studies of team building teachings.

1: No one cares how much you know until they know how much you care.

2: Team members enjoy being around people that can connect with them.

3: Relationship is the bond that holds teams together, the more soiled the association is; the stronger the bond that holds a team together!

4: Just about everything depends on teamwork; so make team work, work for you.

5: Ask yourself this question. Will your participation with others be successful?

6: Your best chance for leadership also depends upon connecting with those on your team.

7: **RESPECT**: When it comes to associations, everything begins with respect, and a desire to see people with great values. The thing about respect is that you should show it to others, even before they have done anything to deserve it or before you know them. But at the same time, you should always expect to have to earn it from others. The place you earn it the quickest is on difficult ground. Team leaders should lead with influence that is of a quality nature.

8: *Experience*: It takes time to share work or task experiences. But to build or improve a team, Leaders and Team Mates must do this. Remember "I learn and it shows". It requires sharing experiences over time and that's not always easy to achieve. If you or your team mates don't share experience your team will not grow fast; this will cause you and the team a lot of time.

9: *Trust*: It takes time and respect to build trust! When you respect people you are developing trust. When you share the work or task experience, you are in a position to develop trust. Trust is necessary to all good relationships. This is what builds great teams. Without trust you cannot sustain any kind of relationship from your co-workers or team mates.

10: ***You can't be a team by yourself***: Team mates and co-workers must learn to work together; not alone, unless it's a small task or it just needs one person. The team is always aware of all small tasks. You don't need a team member that is always the giver or a team member that is always the receiver; this type of team mate will eventually disintegrate them self or deteriorate the team. You don't need to carry the load by yourself either.

11: ***Mutual Enjoyment***: How are you doing when it comes to being relational? Do you spend a lot of time and energy building relationships, or are you so focused on results that you tend to overlook (or overrun) each other?

One's achievements!
There will be a few things that bring you great pleasure in life.
One area of this should be; the time and trouble it takes to understand people around you.
This will add more to your life than anything else.
This will bring you more happiness and greater achievement than anything else.
When we give respect; we are build relationship. The value we place on other people should be real. A great team has great team mates.

By: Bill Carter December 2007
While in Iraq

Notes for team building:

_____
_____
_____
_____
_____
_____
_____
_____
_____
_____
_____
_____
_____
_____
_____
_____
_____
_____
_____
_____
_____
_____
_____
_____

Leadership and Ministry

I'm only going to touch base on a few areas of the Bible, to show you what **Identifies Leadership Qualities.** You can take the time to read into each one of these passages. *If you want to be a leader in your church, you must have the will to study and learn on your own!* <u>Excellent Scripture for leadership to know and live by.</u>

<u>**1 Samuel 16: 7**</u> But the Lord said unto Samuel, Look not on his countenance, or on the height of his stature; because I have refused him: *for the Lord seeth not as man seeth; for man looketh on the outward appearance, but the Lord looketh on the heart*

<u>**Psalm 3:4**</u> *But know that the Lord hath set apart him that is godly for Himself:* the Lord will hear when you call unto him.

<u>**Acts 6:3**</u> Wherefore, brethren, *look ye out among you seven men of honest report, full of the Holy Ghost and wisdom, whom we may appoint over this business.*

<u>**1 Corinthians 1: 26 to 31**</u> (To save time you can read this passage, I just want to point out verse 26: *For ye see your calling brethren, how that not many wise men after the flesh, not many mighty, not many noble, are called:*

<u>**Acts 10:22**</u> And they said, Cornelius the centurion, *a just man, and one that feareth God, and of good report among all the nation of the Jews,* was warned from God by a holy angel to send for thee into his house, and to hear words of thee.

<u>**Acts 11:19 to 30**</u> (Read this passage, The Church in Antioch (**Barnabas**) verse 24: *For he was a good man, and full of the Holy Ghost and of faith: and much people was added unto the Lord.*

<u>**1 Timothy 5:7 to 25**</u> (Read this passage, Duty to elders) verse 7: *Let the elders that rule well be counted worthy of double honor, especially they who labor in the word and doctrine.*

<u>**1 Timothy 3: 1 to 13**</u> (vs. 1 to 7 *Qualifications of a Bishop* / vs. 8 to 13 *Qualifications of Deacons,* **Read and study this passage.**)

<u>**James 2:14 to 26**</u> (Read and study this passage, *Faith that Works.*) Vs. 23 *And the scripture was filled which saith, ABRAHAM BELIEVED GOD, AND IT WAS IMPUTED UNTO HIM FOR RIGHTEOUSNESS: and he was called the Friend of God.*

<u>**Proverbs 8**</u> (Read this whole chapter, *Wisdom is everlasting.*) Vs. 7 and 8: *For my mouth shall speak truth; and wickedness is an abomination to my lips. All the words of my mouth are in righteousness; there is nothing forward or perverse in them.* **(Read Proverbs 6: 16 to 19.)**

An overview from the verse given from above:
But the Lord looketh on the heart * The Lord hath set apart him or her that is godly for Himself
Men & Women of honest report * Full of the Holy Ghost and wisdom
You're called * A just Man or Woman * Fears God * Good report among people
A good person * Great Faith * Can add people to the Church and to the Lord
Labor in the Word and Doctrine * Speaks the Truth * Righteousness
A Friend of God
(Ask and pray that the Holy Spirit will give you insight into each of these)
<u>**Leaders Understands**</u>

Authority

There is only one over the house of God, the Pastor. The Pastor delegates leadership to them that are called. We must learn this: Authority is our friend * Authority in Unity, (this will cause Great Faith and the works of Faith) * Authority loves and Forgives (this will cause the church to grow)

Authority is a Servant, (it gives and works with needs) Authority Knows, (wisdom and knowledge).

Highly Productive people

They understand time management * They study and know (whatever they're doing) * They know what needs to be done (they take care of it, they delegate it out) * They keep things running * They drive toward the goal * They can fix problems * They will talk about their mistakes and problems they can't solve with their leaders * They are not High maintenance people *

They are low Maintenance people * They are organized

Family

Must know that their family is first * Must have enough time to spend with his or her family Should apply great family values all the time

Idealist

One guided by ideals * One that places ideals before practical considerations *
One who listens * One who brain storms

Delegates

Must realize he or she cannot do everything * Must know how and to whom to delegate

Goal Setter

Must have goals * Goals written out for the team to see and understand *
They must be realistic * Goals must have time frames *
Must realize if goals can't be met

Role Model

Can People really look up to you? * Do you live what you teach?
Do you love and forgive? * Do you give and server?

Handing your Leadership over at a due time:

A great leader will have someone in line to hand over his leadership to. A great leader will train one or more leaders, to step in his place as needed or when it's time to hand it over. This is the greatest sign of a Great Leader.

By: Evangelist Bill Carter
7/6/03

Notes for Leadership:

_____

_____

_____

_____

_____

_____

_____

_____

_____

_____

_____

_____

_____

_____

_____

_____

_____

_____

_____

_____

_____

_____

_____

_____

_____

_____

_____

_____

_____

_____

_____

_____

_____

_____

_____

_____

Guide lines for open group meetings

The first thing we need to remember when we work with a group, we must allow God to move through your troubles. Open your Bible to

MATTHEW 11: 28-30 *COME UNTO ME, ALL YE THAT LABOR AND ARE HEAVY LADEN, AND I WILL GIVE YOU REST. VS 29: TAKE MY YOKE UPON YOU, AND LEARN OF ME; FOR I AM MEEK AND LOWLY IN HEART: AND YE SHALL FIND REST UNTO YOUR SOULS. VS 30: FOR MY YOKE IS EASY, AND MY BURDEN IS LIGHT.*

I would like to lay out some guidelines for open group meetings.

1: **Realize that trust grows over time**: you may find some people willing to discuss and others will take their time in building up there trust. But encourage everyone to be a part of the group. Talk to the group about building up their trust.

ISAIAH 26:4 *TRUSTS YE IN THE LORD FOREVER: FOR IN THE LORD JEHOVAH IS EVERLASTING STRENGTH.*

When people don't want to talk, understand that *(talking can seem risky to them!)* Let them know that they don't have to share anymore than they want to. This is the first step in building trust. When a person starts trusting and taking the risk of speaking; they will find, **this as a necessary part of recovery!**
Everyone in the group needs to be a part of all discussions *(as much as they are able to be.)* Yes, a person can take their time in group recovery or studies.

THE LEADER MUST KEEP THE MEETING MOVING!

2: **1 PETER 5:6-8** *HUMBLE YOURSELVES THEREFORE UNDER THE MIGHTY HAND OF GOD, THAT HE MAY EXALT YOU IN DUE TIME: VS 7: CASTING ALL YOUR CARE UPON HIM; FOR HE CARETH FOR YOU. VS 8: BE SOBER, BE VIGILANT; BECAUSE YOUR ADVERSARY THE DEVIL, AS A ROARING LION, WALKETH ABOUT, SEEKING WHOM HE MAY DEVOUR:*

Remember to be sensitive to other members of the group. Make sure you listen when other members are speaking. *You just might hear something!* We can learn from others insight and problems. As well, see if you can connect to their comments. Or see if their comments will give you confidence to talk or give insight to your problems.

3: **PROVERBS 15:23** *A MAN (MANKIND) HATH JOY BY THE ANSWER OF HIS MOUTH: AND A WORD SPOKEN IN DUE SEASON (IN ITS TIME), HOW GOOD IS IT!*
PROVERBS 15: 31 *THE EAR THAT HEARETH THE REPROOF OF LIFE ABIDETH AMONG THE WISE.*

Sometimes we don't mean to; but we can over talk in an open discussion. If you are eager to share what you have on your mind or heart. Learn to do so when there is time or in the right timing. We must learn to leave opportunity for others to respond. But by all means participate.

4: **2 TIMOTHY 2:15-16** *STUDY TO SHOW THYSELF APPROVED UNTO GOD, A WORKER THAT NEEDTH NOT TO BE ASHAMED, RIGHTLY DIVIDING THE WORD OF TRUTH. VS 16: BUT SHUN PROFANE AND VAIN BABBLINGS: FOR THEY WILL INCREASE UNTO MORE UNGODLINESS.*
2 TIMOTHY 1:7-8 *FOR GOD HATH NOT GIVEN US THE SPIRIT OF FEAR; BUT OF POWER, AND OF LOVE, AND OF A SOUND MIND. VS 8: BE NOT THOU THEREFORE ASHAMED OF THE TESTIMONY OF OUR LORD, NOR OF ME HIS PRISONER: BUT BE THOU PARTAKER OF THE AFFLICTIONS OF THE GOSPEL ACCORDING TO THE POWER OF GOD:*

You must expect God to move and teach you through the passages being discussed. The Holy Spirit is our teacher. God can use these types of meetings to move the Holy Spirit and to teach us.

5: **1 CORINTHIANS 4:33** *FOR GOD IS NOT THE AUTHOR OF CONFUSION (DISORDER), BUT OF PEACE, AS IN ALL CHURCHES OF THE SAINTS.*

Leaders must keep the spirit of confusion out of all group meetings. The leader must always stay on track with the topic of the discussion. ***Even if the leader has to stop the meeting to get it back in order! Remember the leader should be lead by the Holy Spirit. This is why the leader must not let the spirit of confusion enter into the meeting or group (people)!*** We must do this with peace. The people; must allow this leader to take charge over the spirit of confusion! This must be done by the leaders only.

THESE GUIDE LINES SHOULD BE READ AT THE START OF THE PROGRAM!

A: <u>Confidential</u>: **What is discussed in the group stays in the group!** <u>**Never discuss what happens or what is said in any group discussions!**</u>
This is a good way to build someone's trust. People need someone to trust and this is a good way for you to help! In order for someone to open up; they must build trust within the group. For all we may know a person has kept this information inside of them for years. When they let something like this out; it's going to hurt and there may be tears. Look at this verse:

PSALM 126:5 *THEY THAT SOW IN TEARS SHALL REAP JOY.*

B: **Proved time for each person:** If he or she feels comfortable in speaking let them speak. If they don't feel like speaking just let someone else speak. If no one wants to speak, this is a good time to talk about one of your testimonies.

PSALM 119:167-168 *MY SOUL HATH KEPT THY TESTIMONIES; AND I LOVE THEM EXCEEDINGLY. VS 168: I HAVE KEPT THY PRECEPTS AND TESTIMONIES: FOR ALL MY WAYS ARE BEFORE THEE.* In these two verses; we see why as leaders should have their testimonies ready. This will help others in the future. ***A good leader will be able to share their testimony, as the Holy Spirit leads them, amen!***

C: <u>**Avoid conversation about other people:**</u> Never name, names! Talk only about ourselves. Which concerns the topic or situations of discussion? This will save time and build trust. Gossiping will only destroy the meetings. This will also tear down trust!

<u>**Psalm 34:13**</u> *Keep Thy Tongue From Evil, And Thy Lips From Speaking Guile (Deceit).*

D: <u>**Let people know that you're listening to them, as they talk**</u>.
Remember this is a chance for that person to open up and build trust. When someone starts talking, they just might be rebuilding their life. Check and see if you hear something that might help you to help them.
Or this may give you something to pray about. But keep this prayer to yourself. God will allow someone to hear the needs of a prayer. So as you listen and wait, let the Holy Spirit move to the speaker and listeners.

E: <u>**PSALM 118:8-9**</u> *IT IS BETTER TO TRUST IN THE LORD THAN TO PUT CONFIDENCE IN MAN. IT IS BETTER TO TRUST IN THE LORD THAN TO PUT CONFIDENCE IN PRINCES.*

Be very cautious about giving advice. You may not mean to, but you could make things worse. So you just might want to keep your thoughts to yourself. Let the Leader direct!
For this reason, every group (recovery & study) has a leader. That leader may have placed people in the group to work in the gift of helps (1 cor. 12:38). Or there may be people of the ministry setting in open groups like: Apostles, Prophets, Evangelists, Pastors, and Teachers.

Now I'm going to show you why the people of the ministry and them that work in the gift of helps, can do a greater work.

<u>**EPHESIANS 4:12-13**</u> *FOR THE PERFECTING OF THE SAINTS, FOR THE WORK OF THE MINISTRY, FOR THE EDIFYING OF THE BODY OF CHRIST: TILL WE ALL COME IN THE UNITY OF FAITH, AND OF THE KNOWLEDGE OF THE SON OF GOD, UNTO A PERFECT MAN, UNTO THE MEASURE OF STATURE OF THE FULLNESS OF CHRIST:*

F: <u>**We will pray for each other**</u>. This is another way to build up trust. But let the leader of the group choose who will pray for the people of the group. The leader has an insight to those who have the same problem.
So never feel bad if you're not asked to pray. I know people sometimes get upset when they feel the need to pray with someone and don't. But, remember who the leader is and why that person was placed there. (Read James 5:7-18 & 5:16).

Make note for Open Group Meetings:

_____
_____
_____
_____
_____
_____
_____
_____
_____
_____
_____
_____
_____
_____
_____
_____
_____
_____
_____
_____
_____
_____
_____
_____
_____
_____
_____
_____
_____
_____
_____
_____
_____
_____
_____

Before you give up

One word of advice I give to people is, "you must have a **Vision**, and make a list of **Goals."** Most Christian doesn't have a vision nor do they set goals. Sometimes people give up before their visions or goals can produce fruit. I'm going to show you a parable that Jesus spoke of in the book of Luke.

Luke 13:6-10 *Vs. 6: **He (Jesus) spake also this parable**; A certain man had a fig tree planted in his vineyard; and he came and sought fruit thereon, and found none.*

A certain man had a fig tree planted: when he planted the fig tree, he planted it to produce fruit. **That was Faith in operation. Remember this, you must have faith. Without faith it's impossible to please God our Father!**

Vs. 7: Then said he (the certain, man) unto the dresser (or keeper) of his vineyard, Behold, these three years I come seeking fruit on this fig tree, why cumbereth (or, does it use up or waste) it the ground.

This **certain man** is expecting his **Harvest or his Vision or Goals to come to pass**. What happened when this fig tree didn't produce any fruit? He was going to **cut down the tree** and **destroy it.**
In other words, **he lost his Faith** and **entered into doubt!** This is what happens to most Christians **when we let doubt, influence our Faith**. What happens when this occurs? **We can lose our Faith; we can destroy our Vision and Goals**. If you keep your Faith between you and God our Father, what will happen? **With God our Father all things are possible!**

Vs.8: And he (the keeper) answering said unto him, Lord (or master of the vineyard), let it alone this year also, till I (the keeper) shall dig about it, and dung it.

What did the **Keeper** say unto the **Master of the vineyard**? *Let it alone!* He had to have **Faith** to say this! He also had **Knowledge and Wisdom** here in this verse. He knew if he *dug around the base or roots he could put dung or fertilize to help the fig tree produce fruit. This is where his knowledge and wisdom came into play. (I want you to take notice of one more thing in this verse. The keeper asked for one more season or year so the fig tree could have a chance to bear fruit).*
vs. 9: And if it bear fruit, well: and if not, then after that thou shalt cut it down.

Look how he placed the word **well**. Jesus said; well *before not in this verse*. Why? The Keeper had Faith with Action. Remember Faith without Action is dead. Faith with Action pleases our Father, in whom all things are possible!
Vs. 10: And he (Jesus) was teaching in one of the synagogues on the Sabbath.

This is a teaching to all of the believers or Christian. Where was he teaching this? In the Synagogues on the Sabbath. Why was Jesus Christ teaching this? To keep your Faith alive in your harvest, Vision, and Goals!

I want you to keep in mind what you need to receive your harvest or keep your Vision and Goals alive:

1: Faith
2: Keep doubt out of your Faith
3: You may need someone else to help or their Faith to be involved
4: Give one more season or year, or give it more time
5: You must have Knowledge and Wisdom
6: Faith with Action produces greater Faith
7: You must believe that all things are possible with God our Father

Note: And above all, Faith without action is dead. Remember this, it may take few years or more to reach your harvest or Vision or Goals! Above all things stay in the Word of God (keep reading and studying your Bible) and don't stop praying, Amen!

By: Evangelist Bill Carter
5/6/03

Goals

We as Christians can set the pace of life if we have goals. Do you have goals? I believe, we should have short term and long term goals. If you thought hard enough, I know you could have at least ten to fifteen goals.

HABAKKUK 2:2 *THE LORD ANSWERED ME, AND SAID, WRITE THE VISION, AND MAKE IT PLAIN UPON TABLES **(or tablets or paper)**, THAT HE MAY RUN THAT READETH IT.*

Look at this verse, **what is it telling you?** The Lord is telling us to write down our vision **(or goals).** Make it plain upon tablets or paper. **This means to put it in order, to know what you want!** That he may run that readeth it. Who is reading this vision or goal? What does this mean to you? That he may run that readeth it. We must take action in our vision or goals. Not only in prayer but action, but we must know without faith our action is dead. We must keep our vision alive in prayer, faith and action!

PROVERBS 29:18 *WHERE THERE IS NO VISION, THE PEOPLE PERISH: BUT HE THAT KEEPETH THE LAW, HAPPY IS HE.*

Let's take a look at this verse. It starts off, where there is no vision. This is telling us what happens, the people perish. See what happens if we don't have visions or goals! We just perish.

What happens when we keep this law? Happy is he or she. Why does this make us happy? If, we have something to run to with faith and action; God is blessing us, amen.

PSALM 37:4-5 *DELIGHT THYSELF ALSO IN THE LORD; AND HE SHALL GIVE THEE THE DESIRES OF THINE HEART. VS. 5: COMMIT (loving-kindness) THY WAY UNTO THE LORD; TRUST ALSO IN HIM; AND HE SHALL BRING IT TO PASS.*

First of all if you and I are Christians, we must delight ourselves in the lord, amen. If we give our all to the Lord, what will God return to you? He (God) shall give thee the desires of your heart. But, we must commit our ways to the Lord. Trusting in God to bring your goals into reality. Once again, faith with action!

GALATIANS 6:9 AND *LET US NOT BE WEARY IN WELL DOING: FOR IN DUE SEASON WE SHALL REAP, IF WE FAINT NOT.*

And let us not be weary in well doing. This is stating, that it may take, patience and time. For in due season, we shall receive (or reap). If we faint not; faint not means not to give up. **This is why we must believe in our faith, in God. With prayer, faith, and action.**

I'm not going to break down these next two verses in Hebrews. But, I would like to ask you to read it a few times. There is a Godly power, in Jesus. That stands out in a way that brings our faith together in Jesus Christ, amen!

HEBREWS 12:1-2 *WHEREFORE SEEING WE ALSO ARE COMPASSED ABOUT WITH SO GREAT A CLOUD OF WITNESSES, LET US LAY ASIDE EVERY WEIGHT, AND THE SIN WHICH DOTH SO EASILY BESET US, AND LET US RUN WITH PATIENCE THE RACE THAT IS SET BEFORE US, VS. 2: LOOKING UNTO JESUS THE AUTHOR AND FINISHER OF OUR FAITH; WHO FOR THE JOY THAT WAS SET BEFORE HIM ENDURED THE CROSS, DESPISING THE SHAME, AND IS SET DOWN AT THE RIGHT HAND OF THE THRONE OF GOD.*

I can't tell you how much you need to have goals or visions in your life. **With goals there is a race to be won, and a blessing to be received.** Without goals you will become unhappy and life may just pass you by. Please write down your goals, you may have to change some of your goals; and as you fulfill your goals make new ones. Keep focused on your goals. Your goals should be specific, measurable, realistic, timed, and written. May the lord bless your visions and goals, amen!

OBSTACLES ARE WHAT YOU SEE
WHEN YOU TAKE YOU'RE MIND
OFF OF YOUR
GOALS

By: Evangelist Bill Carter 3/14/01

THE TEST OF LIFE

What happens when we have a test in our life? A lot goes on as we walk through this life. How do we get through this test? One could say one day at a time with Jesus, Amen! As I have listened to some Pastors that are filled with wisdom and the Holy Spirit, the Holy Spirit has given me some insight on the test of life.

Pastor / Dr. Ed Davis was talking to me one day, about when he taught a vocational school. His statement stuck in my mind. God dealt with me over this issue for a week. Then I went to a church in Hartford, Ky. to hear Pastor Richard Curtis. I didn't know that he gave me a word that would add to Pastor Davis statement. But God took two Pastors to reveal this to me.

How do we get prepared for a test? What does it take? How do you know if you pass the test?

ATTITUDE/ STUDY/ TEST

Our *Attitude* is 60% of our test. *Study* is 20% & *Test* is 20%. This is your 100%

Attitude: *Philippians2:5* *Let this mind be in you, which was also in Christ Jesus.* **(This mind = Christ like Attitude).**

Study: *2 Timothy 2:15* *Study to show thyself approved unto God,* **(If you study in this manner, you will receive wisdom and knowledge from God)!**

Test: *1Peter 1:7* *That the trial of you faith, being much more precious than of gold that perisheth, though it be tried with fire, might be found unto praise and honor and glory at the appearing of Jesus Christ:* **(Trial of faith = Test / This is more precious than Gold)!**

I know that God has given me something that is deep in my soul. Bear this in mind; this is for all Christians that have walked in faith. Now let me show you the rest of what God has given me:

*Let's leave **Attitude** as the same word **Attitude**. The word **Study** and look at it, as if it were the word **accountable**. The word **Test** as if it were the word **Faith.** This is the way we get 110% and how we pass **The Test of Life.***

ATTITUDE / STUDY/ TEST
ATTITUDE / ACCOUNTABLE / FAITH
(This gives us 110%)

What causes us to fail? This happens when there is no Progress!

James 2:20 *But wilt thou know, O vain man, that faith without works is dead?* **(There we have it, faith without works is dead, and this is where there is no progress)!**

James 2:26 *For as the body without the spirit is dead, so faith without works is dead also.* **(We must keep our spirit alive in Christ, and our faith in Christ full of action = Progress)!**

Progress: *2 Timothy 4:7* *I have fought a good fight, I have finished my course, I have Kept the faith.* **(You have got to fight a good fight, finish the course and keep the faith)!**

By: Evangelist Bill Carter 12/30/02

MY PRAYER TO YOU

May this writing be a blessing to all the people that reads this book!
We all know about broken hearts.
It's my prayer that this will heal the ones with broken hearts.
May you reach out to God our father; in all of your needs!
May God bless your needs!
This is a time to rebuild your life as a single adult.
Let your faith change your life to the way of Christ.
Teach us to lift up each other in times of need.
Father this hour I ask and pray that you heal all that are broken hearted.
Let their life be filled with your love.
Lord, send them their soul mate even as we pray!
Lord, we give you thanks in all things.
I ask that this prayer be answered by all that reads this,
In the name of Jesus Christ,
AMEN!

IF YOU WISH TO SUPPORT THIS WRITING MINISTRY
WITH YOUR LOVE GIFTS
PLEASE SEND YOUR LOVE GIFTS
TO
BILL CARTER
PO BOX 1602
OWENSBORO, KY 42302
USA

MY GOAL FOR THIS WRITING, IS TO REACH
MILLIONS OF SINGLE ADULTS
THIS IS A GREAT BOOK FOR ALL SINGLE ADULTS
A book to help you, your friends, and loved one's

Peace After Your Broken Relationship

SEEDS OF FAITH ALWAYS GROW

There are over fifty short subjects in this book
That relates to relationship development.
This book is to help you overcome your past.
It will help you begin a great future.
This is a great book to hand out,
It could help someone overcome a past relationship.

For: Single Adults & Teaching Groups
OPEN GROUP RECOVERY
Leadership teaching for open group leaders

*First part of a broken relationship * I'm still in love * Dealing with rejection*
*Dealing with anger * Attitude * Anxiety * Fear * Bitterness * Guilt*
*Loneliness * Revenge * Shame * Depression * Thanksgiving*
*Self Control * Gossip * Assurance * Speaking Openly*
*Sin Factor * Fantasy * Getting over the hurt * Forget and move on*
Don't mess up someone's life Praying for your soul mate*
*Love / Friend * Relationship Commitment * Friendship or Love*
*On trail for love * Love for a reason ***
*Imaginary Relationship * So involved you don't see the truth*
*Love on the job * Mistakes * Changing for a better relationship*
*Easily Offended * Conflict in your relationship * Reconciling*
*Our expectation of people * Communication * Argue*
*Never love anyone more than God * Divorce*
*Why I love you * Relationship * Trail of faith*

Each subject is given to make you think about yourself and others.
I pray that this book will reach millions of single adults!